Walking Where We Lived

Walking Where We Lived

Memoirs of a Mono Indian Family

By Gaylen D. Lee
Foreword by Mark Q. Sutton

University of Oklahoma Press : Norman

This book is published with
the generous assistance of
Edith Gaylord Harper.

Library of Congress Cataloging-in-Publication Data

Lee, Gaylen D. (Gaylen Dennis), 1949–
    Walking where we lived: memoirs of a Mono Indian family / Gaylen
D. Lee.
      p. cm.
    Includes bibliographical references and index.
    ISBN 0-8061-3087-3 (alk. paper)
    1. Mono Indians. 2. Moore family. I. Title.
E99.M86L44   1998
979.4'004974—dc21   98-13492
                                                        CIP

The paper in this book meets the guidelines for permanence and durability of the Committee on Production Guidelines for Book Longevity of the Council on Library Resources, Inc.♾

2   3   4   5   6   7   8   9   10

From Chauwahiniu I walk
crying I walk
looking for my people.
I see no one anymore.
I walk crying, "Poor little thing."
Walking where they lived
walking over their graves
but see no one.
　　　　　—Willie Pomona's personal song

CONTENTS

ILLUSTRATIONS

PHOTOGRAPHS

MAPS

FOREWORD

In this memoir, Gaylen Lee recounts the personal history of his Nɨm (North Fork Mono) family across six generations. He also brings to light the treatment, problems, and survival of the Nɨm in general. This is a view that most never see: the perspective of American Indians themselves on their own culture, traditions, and condition. We can learn much about the Nɨm from Gaylen's account. We can also learn that there are things outsiders are not to know—a difficult reality for the ever-curious student of human behavior but one that must be respected.

Walking Where We Lived takes us through the yearly cycle of the Nɨm. Beginning with spring—a time of renewal and life—the memoir then moves through summer, fall, and winter, then back again to spring. The end of the book returns to the beginning, just as each spring is a repetition of the last. Thus the reader, along with the Nɨm, is brought full circle into a new year. The memoir itself may be viewed as the beginning of a new spring, a time when the Nɨm are being renewed through the efforts of Gaylen and others to preserve the way of the people.

Gaylen's memoir is important because it is the first published account of the Nɨm written by a representative of this group. Until now, our knowledge of the Nɨm has been based largely on the work of anthropologists. Anthropological interest in the Nɨm, considered part of a larger group known as the Western Mono (or Monache, Monachi, or Monos), has a relatively long history. Most early studies were summarized by Robert F. G. Spier in *California,* volume 8 of the *Handbook of North American Indians* (1978), including the work of Anna H. Gayton, A. L. Kroeber, Harold Driver, and Edward W. Gifford. A new generation of researchers continues to work with the Mono.

Most of the information provided by Gaylen complements and adds to what has been learned by anthropologists. Some information corrects their errors. For instance, Gaylen shows how translations of Nɨm songs into English sometimes misrepresent their meaning. More significantly, he reveals the ways in which anthropologists have misunderstood ceremonies and ceremonial intent. There are also areas where anthropologists and the Nɨm will not agree. For example, the standard anthropological view is that Native peoples migrated into America from Asia some twelve thousand years ago and that the Nɨm entered their current territory sometime within the last one thousand years. The Nɨm do not believe this, instead claiming the region as their place of origin. This disagreement highlights differences in perspective.

I have known the Lee family for a number of years and learn from them each time we visit. Learning is a slow process, even under ideal conditions, for the accumulated knowledge of the Nɨm is extensive and complex. That Gaylen and his family have chosen to share some of it will benefit us all. I am honored to be their friend.

MARK Q. SUTTON

Bakersfield, California

ACKNOWLEDGMENTS

In pursuing the historical context of the advancing civilization's effect on my family I am indebted to the following people: Cheryl McClure, librarian of the North Fork branch; Ruth Vandenack, librarian-technician, interlibrary loan; and Sue Rhu, librarian of the Oakhurst branch, Madera County Library, California, were instrumental in locating valuable historical material from throughout California. The North Fork branch library is also a repository for the California Indian Library Collection, made available by the Lowie Museum of Anthropology, University of California, Berkeley.

Others who provided access to historical material are Connie Popelish, archaeologist at the Minarets Ranger District, USDA Forest Service, Sierra National Forest, North Fork, California; Karen G. Miller, forest archaeologist for the Sierra National Forest, Clovis, California; Terry Boom, project archivist, C. Hart Merriam Collection, The Bancroft Library, University of California, Berkeley; Joseph Schwarz, Archival Programs Branch, Center for Leglislative Archives, National Archives, Washington, D.C.; Ron Mahoney, Department of Special Collections, Henry Madden Library, California State University, Fresno; Stephanie Muntone, processing archivist for the Presbyterian Historical Society, Philadelphia, Pennsylvania; and Linda Eade, librarian, Research Library, Yosemite National Park.

Thanks to Gail Fain, Erica Liederman Rex, Rob Russell, and Jacquie Davis Van Huss. Thanks also to John Drayton, editor-in-chief, Alice K. Stanton, associate editor, Randolph Lewis, acquisitions editor, and Patsy Willcox, production manager, at the University of Oklahoma Press, for their suggestions and guidance; and to Sheila Berg, copy editor, for her sensitive approach to the manuscript.

William Scheidt shared his maps from an independent research project in the Hensley Lake area where the Fresno River Farm was located; Ross Peckinpah drew the map of the Moore family homeland; Edwin Daubs, retired biology and environmental science professor at California State University, Fresno, helped me identify plants whose names I knew only in the Nɨm language; Mary Myers, Frank and Isobel Seeley, Sue Rhu, Mark and Melinda Sutton, Mom, and Aunt Ethel read the manuscript and offered suggestions.

When my grandmother, Margaret Moore Bobb, was a young woman she acquired a small camera and became the family's photographer. She was always taking pictures, Mom said. Many of them appear in this book, thanks to Glen Bredon's expertise. Glen also prepared other family photographs and additional photographs from private collections for publication in this book.

Evan J. Norris was pursuing a B.A. degree in linguistics when I met him at California State University, Fresno, in 1974. He devised the linguistic symbols that I use when writing the Nɨm language. Thank you, Evan, wherever you are.

My wife, Judy Barras Lee, did the research that fleshed out my family's oral traditions of historical events. Her love of history is evident in her exhaustive and extensive research over several years that resulted in the historical perspective of my family's life.

My mother, Ruby Pomona, was a major contributor to this book. We talked often during the last few years about the past, our way of life, and her childhood memories. This is her story as much as it is mine. She has my deepest love and appreciation.

Walking Where
We Lived

KEY TO
DIACRITICAL MARKS

a = a as in father
e = e as in bet
i = ee as in feet
o = o as in boat
u = oo as in boot
ai = i as in kite
k = c as in cat
ɨ = u as in put
´ = stops a vowel sound as in uh-oh!
: = extended vowel sounds as in
    o: = boooo
    a: = baaaa

CHAPTER ONE

INTRODUCTION

My name is Taʼa:kai. I am a descendant of Cha:tiniu Nɨm, who lived deep in California's Sierra Nevada near the San Joaquin River. Our family lived there in the 1850s, when only Indians lived in its dense forests. The name Cha:tiniu is not found on any maps; it is a meadow of considerable size about forty-five miles from the village of North Fork in Madera County, California.

My grandparents, Margaret Moore Bobb, whose Nɨm name is Tuhɨwɨ, and Charlie "Hotshot" Moore, whose Nɨm name is Sakɨma, are identified throughout this book as Grandma and Grandpa. Although they died within months of each other in 1981, they remain a presence in my life. All that I say, speak, see, feel, do, all that I am, is because of their influence, and my mother's; and, indirectly, because of so many other relatives of my grandparents' generation who never hesitated to teach and counsel me during my youth.

Grandpa never married. Grandma married Jim Bobb, a Chukchansi Yokuts from Coarsegold. Grandpa and Grandma were actually brother and sister to my biological grandmother, Emma Moore Pomona, who died when her daughters, Ruby and Ethel, were children; and they were uncle and aunt to my mother, Ruby Pomona,

Charlie "Hotshot" Moore
in the mid-1950s.
(Author's collection)

and to her sister, Ethel Pomona Temple. In our tradition, in the absence of living biological grandparents, they were Grandma and Grandpa to me and my sister, Gloria.

The structure of our language supports close family ties: the Nɨm appellative *piya* is used by a child when referring to its mother or her sister (or sisters). That's why I refer to those known by non-Indians as great-uncles and great-aunts as Grandpa and Grandma plus their given English name.

Also, according to our tradition, Grandpa and Grandma, as Grandma Emma's siblings, eventually raised to adulthood the Pomona girls and, at different times, their first cousins, Herb and Harvey Punkin, whose mother, Daisy Moore Punkin, another of Grandpa's and Grandma's siblings, died when the boys were children.

Grandpa is my hero. He was the only father I knew, sharing with me the old ways, the life of my family as it was lived in traditional times, before other races came to our land. He showed me how to live the old way and, at the same time, live in the present. As Grandpa aged, it was hard for him to walk. After my uncles, Herb and Harvey Punkin, left home when I was in my preteens, there wasn't anyone to provide food for the family. Grandpa decided to teach me how to hunt and fish, how to dress meat, and how to make traditional hunting tools.

Grandma was my mentor. She encouraged me to walk the white man's path, while at the same time she and Grandpa taught me how to be a man in the old way. Their teaching wasn't structured but spontaneous, as we lived day-to-day. I had no idea then that I was being taught a unique lifestyle. My classroom was every-where, all the time. I learned my ancestors' songs and stories that have been shared from generation to generation; they taught, among other things, how to care for and share with everyone and everything.

Mom continues to live in the house where I was raised, a stone's throw from my own home off of Cascadel Road, about two miles east of North Fork. After my grandparents took their dead sisters' children to raise in the mid-1940s, their brother, John Moore, built a small two-room frame cabin on what was then U.S. Forest Service land. By the time I was born, Grandpa John had enlarged the orig-inal cabin to several rooms.

I have vivid memories of snuggling next to Grandma each night in one of the bedrooms, while Gloria and Mom shared a bed in an-other room. Grandpa lived alone in a small cabin he built nearby, but he always ate with us and shared the family's activities. Our fam-ily continued to preserve the tradition of extended family nurturing.

It wasn't until I began Fresno Community College in the late 1960s that I heard strange notions about the Nɨm. During a fresh-man anthropology class, a professor explained the theory that American Indians of the western United States arrived there in some distant time after a lengthy migration from Asia. Supposedly, these people, while hunting now-extinct giant animals, crossed a

Left, Gaylen Lee in 1975, with his grandmother, Margaret Moore Bobb. She is holding Gaylen's daughter, Jacqueline Lee. (Author's collection)

then-existing landbridge in today's Bering Strait that connected Asia with the North American continent. Over thousands of years, the migrants eventually dispersed southward, into the western United States. I remember raising my arm, being recognized, and correcting the professor. "That's just not true," I declared, and shared the real story of our arrival in the Sierra Nevada, as told to me by Grandma.

> All the animals gathered at Chu:wani, from all over the hills. They talked and danced all night, before they were supposed to fly and become Indian people. The morning came, when they were supposed to fly and go all over the world. They painted themselves with colors of the rainbow, and became the colors that animals have now by dipping their hands in the paint and touching their bodies.

All the animals came out onto a flat open area. Once everyone got there, they sent Coyote down to get water before they flew. "We shall all drink water before we all fly," they agreed. They told one another about which animal they would be. Coyote wanted to be Eagle, so he said, "I'm going to be Eagle and walk around very proud." So everyone said, "Yes." After this, he went down to get the water. He went down in the valley, to the spring. He got the water and started back. As he started up the hill, he saw a huge shadow. He saw the sky blackened by the animals that had started to fly. He set his bucket down and ran fast as he could, over to a high rock. He started to fly, but fell down to the ground. He kept this up for a long while, until he tired. Gopher kept sticking his head out of the ground to see what was going on. Coyote saw him and said he should stay there and eat things on the ground and be like this always. He went after Gopher but was too tired to eat him. He said, "Well, I guess this is the way I'm going to be. I will stay here and eat whatever is here." He did not become a great Eagle. Instead, he became Coyote, who is cunning and fast. All the animals that left populated the world, and either became people, as we are today, or remained animals.

The professor was skeptical, but he encouraged me over the next several weeks to write the stories I had learned from my grandparents. So I did, exactly as they spoke, in English that might curl a teacher's hair. For the sake of propriety, the translations that appear in this book have been edited.

Virtually every book that describes the Western Mono says we are nomadic hunter-gatherers. We're so much more than that. We were, and still are, human beings, so in tune with our natural surroundings that we enjoyed seasonal forays to reap the land's harvest, always returning to our permanent homes for the long winters.

During the so-called Indian Wars of the early 1850s, military guides, who were usually Indians from the San Joaquin Valley, called the Indians who lived in the mountains near the San Joaquin River *mona*. As soldiers, miners, and federal authorities came to

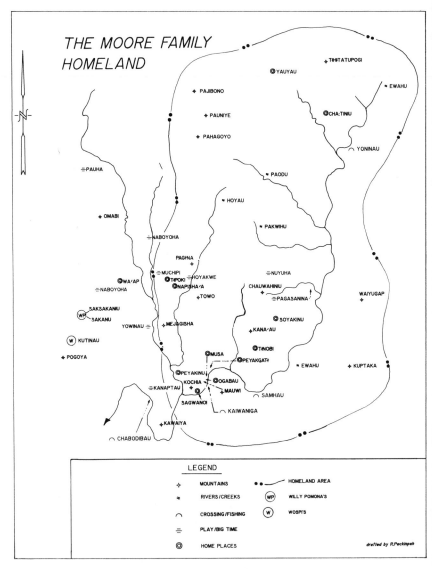

THE MOORE FAMILY HOMELAND

drafted by R.Peckinpah

LEGEND

✦	MOUNTAINS	●●⌒	HOMELAND AREA
≈	RIVERS/CREEKS	(WP)	WILLY POMONA'S
⌒	CROSSING/FISHING	(W)	WOSPI'S
=	PLAY/BIG TIME		
◎	HOME PLACES		

KEY TO MAP

BIG TIME/PLAY AREAS

Cha:tiniu	Logan Meadow
Hoyakwe	Cascadel Woods
Kanaptau	Moore family's Easter Sunday gathering near Redinger Lake
Muchipi	North Fork Recreation Center
Naboyoha	Molly Charlie's home and Herb Punkin's home on Road 274

Nuyuha	Hogue Ranch
Pagasanina	Across from Ross cabin on Minarets Road
Pauha	Bass Lake area
Yowinau	Rex Ranch on Road 222

CROSSING/FISHING PLACES

Chabodibau	Modern-day bridge over San Joaquin River at Auberry Road
Kaiwaniga	East of Redinger Lake Dam on San Joaquin River
Samhau	North of Chawanakee School in the community of Chawanakee
Yoninau	East of San Joaquin River across from Logan Meadow. Now underwater due to Mammoth Pool dam.

HOME PLACES

Cha:tiniu	Logan Meadow
Musa	Moore home west of San Joaquin River
Napisha'a	North Fork Rancheria
Ogabau	East of Redinger Lake near existing power line
Peyakati	Moore home west of San Joaquin River
Peyakinu	Moore home south of Italian Bar Road
Sagwanoi	Moore home west of San Joaquin River
Soyakinu	Kinsman Flat
Tinobi	Moore home near Lion Point
Tipoki	Public domain allotments east of Cascadel Road
Wa'ap	Community of North Fork
Yauyau	Chiquito Basin

MOUNTAINS

Chauwahiniu	Source Point
Kana'au	Lion Point
Kawaiya	Long Ridge
Kochia	Northeast of San Joaquin River near Willow Creek (not identified on modern maps)
Kuptaka	Musick Mountain
Mauwi	West of Redinger Lake (not identified on modern maps)
Mejagisha	West of Whisky Creek bridge on Road 225 (not identified on modern maps)
Omabi	Goat Mountain
Pagina	Peckinpah Mountain
Pahagoyo	Big Shuteye Mountain
Pajibono	Little Shuteye Mountain
Pauniye	Eagle Beaks
Pogoya	Fish Creek
Tihitatupogi	Fuller Buttes
Towo	Cascadel Point
Waiyugap	East of San Joaquin River near Big Creek (not identified on modern maps)

RIVERS/CREEKS

Ewahu	San Joaquin River
Hoyau	Whisky Creek
Pakwihu	Fish Creek
Paodu	Rock Creek

WILLY POMONA'S HOME

Sakanu	Northeast of Fish Creek Mountain
Saksakaniu	Northeast of Fish Creek Mountain

WOSPI'S PLACE

Kutinau	East of Fish Creek Mountain

the region of what is known today as central California, they, too, called the mountain Indians *mona* or *mono*. In the early 1900s, anthropologists also began to identify the Nɨm as Mono, or Monache (and in recent years many Nɨm have done the same).

There are several explanations for the etymology of *mona*. According to Alfred Kroeber, the Indians of the central San Joaquin Valley say that *monai* or *monoyi* means "flies," alluding to the eating of *kuzavi*, small waterborne fly larvae, a practice of Indians near Mono Lake, east of the Sierra Nevada divide. Some Nevada Indian tribes still call Indians living at Mono Lake "kuzavi eaters." The northwestern Maidu word *monazi* is another form of the Yokuts *monachi*, which may also have originated with early trappers who adopted the Pyramid Lake Paviotso word *manats* to describe the Washo Indians of the Lake Tahoe region.[1]

In our language, *mona* describes the action of climbing up something, and the appellative *chi* describes a "special" or "little" friend. If I used *monachi* in a sentence, I could be describing my special friend who lives on the other side of the mountain, after I climbed up. Mom says, "It means top of the hill to the other side."

It is unfortunate that all people who speak the same language are lumped together as either Eastern or Western Mono, suggesting we have the same cultural and aesthetic traits. This is not the case. These traits depend on where one lives and the teachings of individual families.

Neither Grandma nor Grandpa ever identified themselves as Mono or Monache. After moving to their last home off of Cascadel Road near North Fork, when somebody, either Indian or non-Indian, asked them what tribe they were, they replied, "Tɨpoki Nɨm." Tɨpoki is the name of the place where the family has lived since the early 1940s.

Walking Where We Lived is not a deliberate attempt to take issue with those scholars whose research on the Nɨm has been published, among them, Anna Gayton, Edward Gifford, and Sidney Lamb. Their work is listed in the bibliography. Since my family raised and taught me, it is my family's teaching that is revealed in this book; I have only used other material to flesh out historical occurrences alluded to by them.

Also, this book is not intended to be at odds with the thoughts and ideas of other Nɨm. *Walking Where We Lived* is the truth about my family, beginning with the earliest knowledge I have of them when my great-great-great-grandmother, Chinitit, lived at Cha:tiniu. Grandpa John was ninety years old when he described his childhood memory of her: "A little woman, white hair."

I have purposely excluded from this book our concepts of puberty and any individual's "medicine" experiences, as they are, to put it plainly, no one else's business. I describe only those concepts or ceremonies that have already appeared in print, usually grossly misconstrued by non-Indians.

To better understand *Walking Where We Lived* it helps to eliminate from preconceived thought those linear perceptions that govern the Western mind, such as god, creator, spirit, heaven, hell, church, religion, dominion, shaman, totem, moiety/clan (we call them "sides"), and the many other philosophical and anthropological terms too often used when speaking or writing about American Indians. By accepting the possibility of a relationship of all things to each other, there are no boundaries. As Grandma said, "Everything is just the way it is. Just accept it, don't ask why."

The Nɨm language was the only one I spoke when I entered the public school system at six years old. Where a Nɨm word is used in this book it is because I still use it in everyday conversation with other Nɨm speakers. I have used English words to assist non-Indian readers in identifying general areas; I do not give specific locations so as to protect them from trespass and indiscriminate exploitation.

Lest it appear that my family gave in too easily, beginning in the 1850s, to the onslaught of a foreign culture, the reader needs to be aware of an attitude I was taught very early—*aishupa´,* a word that is not easily translated. Grandma would say in broken English, "That's OK. That's all right." As the force of the federal government's doctrine of Manifest Destiny swept through our land, how often our family practiced aishupa´. As Grandma also said, "It all comes around."

It is snowing today, the first major snowfall we've had in North Fork in three years. Snow covers everything. I cannot ignore that this first seasonal snowfall that marks the beginning of winter in our culture occurs on the day I begin writing the final draft of *Walking Where We Lived.* My heart says this isn't a coincidence. My grandparents said stories were to be told only on the snowy days of winter so as to not disturb Rattlesnake, snug in his winter home, because he, in turn, disturbs all other living creatures. Rattlesnake would appear soon enough in spring, they said, when the orange-breasted flicker returned from his southern haunts and began singing to Rattlesnake that the days were warm, and he should come out and enjoy the sunshine.

I miss my grandparents today. Memories of other winter days fill my heart. I still see them, sitting by the wood-burning stove in our snug house, surrounded by the family as they tell the stories of our past and fill our present with continuity.

CHAPTER TWO

LIFE AT CHA:TINIU

High in the fastness of the central Sierra Nevada there are startling contrasts. On a clear day a bright blue sky mantles the land. During stormy weather wild cloud formations hug the peaks as a black sky darkens the landscape and a cacophonous serenade of thunder breaks over one peak, rebounding to another and another. Lightning streaks across the sky, creating a brilliant light show unduplicated by humankind.

Spectacular granite domes thrust upward, towering mountains encircle broad meadows bordered by ancient trees—coniferous pines and cedars, deciduous oaks. The San Joaquin River flows swiftly through this splendid land, tumbling westward in deep canyons from the highest reaches of the Sierra Nevada to the San Joaquin Valley far below, emptying, finally, into the Sacramento Delta.

Chinitit, my great-great-great-grandmother, lived here during the mid-nineteenth century, on the fringe of a large rolling meadow she called Cha:tiniu. Other families lived here too, their conclaves of houses—we call them *tonobi*—embracing extended family groups. The tonobi was made from the bark of *wa´ap*, the cedar tree. Each family group had several tonobi: one for the grandpar-

The impounded San Joaquin River at the modern-day locale of Mammoth Pool dam in California's central Sierra Nevada. Cha:tiniu is a meadow partially visible behind a Ponderosa pine north of the San Joaquin and at the center of the photograph. (Courtesy of Donn Lusby)

ents, another for the grandparents' children and grandchildren, still another for sisters and brothers, perhaps an uncle or aunt or two. It was a lifestyle that assured the continued nurturing and care of everyone in the family, as well as the continuity of traditions. To avoid trampling into destruction the grass and plants growing in the spongy soil of winter and spring, the houses were purposely located at the meadow's edge or on the occasional hummocks of land scattered in the meadow.

Near each cluster of tonobi was at least one sweathouse, shade arbors, windbreaks, racks for drying meat and fish, fire pits for cooking and heat, hitching posts for the horses. There were several granaries for storing acorns, and a large outcropping of granite rock was always nearby, on which shallow depressions developed over time as women pounded acorn nuts from the oak trees. There were also basins for leaching acorn flour.

Mine was a handsome family, the men invariably tall, usually six feet or more, their chests broad, their waists narrow, with no hint of fat. The women, too, were sturdy, though shorter. My ancestors' features varied: some had round faces; others, lean and sculptured. Their hair and eyes were black. Their skin was golden brown.

Both men and women pierced their ears as receptacles for hollow quail bone into which feathers were inserted. Everyone in the same family wore identical facial tattoos of geometric marks. Grandma was the last of Chinitit's descendants to be similarly marked; I recall seeing a faint geometric tattoo on her chin. During a man's daily toilet he used two pieces of clam shell or wood to tweeze off his facial and body hair, because it was considered ugly.

Clothing was minimal and influenced by the weather. Men wore a breechclout and women wore a skirt, both made of deerskin. Both men and women were bare chested, and both usually wore necklaces of strung seashell beads, obtained in trade with coastal Indians. Children didn't wear clothing until they entered puberty. Everyone went barefoot, except in cold weather, when they wore moccasins and wrapped themselves with deerskins or mountain lion skins or robes fashioned from rabbit skins. They wore their hair long and cut straight across the forehead into bangs. And like Lizard, the people had hands with fingers, not paws like Coyote.

> Coyote and Lizard were walking together. Coyote saw a walking stick on the ground. Coyote leaned over to pick it up. He tried and tried, but with no result. Lizard picked the walking stick up. Coyote got angry at his brother, Lizard. "You think you're better than I, huh?" Lizard couldn't believe his brother. Coyote started to boast about how good he was. He stood on his hind legs and started to dance around, singing, "Oh, I am good, I am the leader, all my children will be like me," lifting his paws up to show his brother. Lizard said, "My children will have hands like me. You see this, Coyote, like me." Lizard said, "No, my brother, they will have hands like me," lifting his hand to Coyote. "They will hold things and climb." Coyote grabbed Lizard and threw him down. Lizard rolled Coyote over. Dust was flying. The two brothers fought for hours. Lizard finally threw Coyote into a ditch. Old Coyote gave in and said, "My brother, you have won." Coyote crawled out and under his breath said, "I will get you for this." So this is how all people have hands and fingers like Lizard.   —as told by Grandma

Coyote's name is Isha, and Lizard's is Pogoya.

Pets were common. Grandma said wild animals were tamed sufficiently to handle. *Mauwi,* the gray squirrel, and *tewa,* the cottontail rabbit, lived in wooden cages. Young birds flew freely but were easily coaxed with food to come when called. There was an abundance of tɨhɨt, deer. Unafraid, herds lived so close to people they could be coaxed to eat from a person's hand.

At other places near Cha:tiniu, where large meadows opened beneath the heavy stands of trees, where constant streams and creeks flowed unimpeded over the ground, lived other families who intermarried with Chinitit's kinfolk. Grandma said that some-

Elsie Capp, the author's great-great-grandmother on his mother's maternal side, in the early 1900s. She is holding two of her coiled baskets that are used to store miscellaneous items. On the ground are two coiled baskets that are used to store cooked acorn. (Author's collection)

where nearby (probably across the San Joaquin River, which was Nɨm territory from the Sierra Nevada divide west to just east of Auberry) lived Oposowa, who was Lizzie Moore's, my maternal great-grandmother's, grandfather. Grandma doubted that he had an English name. Great-grandma Lizzie's mother's name was Elsie Capp; I don't know her Nɨm name. Great-grandma Lizzie's Nɨm name was Sihayuni.

Trails, some still visible, crisscrossed the Sierra Nevada then, at places now known as Fine Gold Creek, Italian Bar, Kinsman Flat, Chiquito Basin, and Graveyard Meadow, enabling my ancestors to travel from place to place by foot or on horseback. In some places these trails were bisected by the main trail from the San Joaquin Valley, which began near today's Friant. From Graveyard Meadow, Grandpa said, the family often traveled a trail now called the "old French trail," toward the mountain we know today as Mammoth, to visit friends east of the Sierras, the *sibiti* Nɨm (*sibiti* means "east").

Throughout the western Sierras, on both sides of the San Joaquin River, were other settlements of people who also spoke our language. East of the river, near the modern community of Auberry, were the *unapati* Nɨm (*unapati* means "across"). The *patati* Nɨm (*patati* means "south"), lived to the southwest, in the southern Sierra Nevada foothills.

Beyond our borders, to the west and southwest, in the lower foothills and on the floor of the San Joaquin Valley, still live our immediate neighbors, the Komotini (meaning "river-bottom" Indians). In the old days, they were probably those who called themselves Dalinchi, Toltichi, and Dumna. To the northwest, along the Chowchilla and Fresno rivers, lived the Wowa, who identified themselves as Chukchansi, as they are still called today. Scholars have collectively identified all of these tribes and many other San Joaquin Valley tribes as Yokuts. To the northeast, in the foothills and mountains at and beyond the modern-day village of Ahwahnee, still live the Kosomo, whom scholars identify as Miwok.

Most of these other tribes were enemies. But we maintained a semblance of peace with the Wowa, sufficient to encourage occasional intermarriage and the sharing of the eagle ceremony each spring. Once though, long ago, Grandpa said, the Nɨm defeated the Wowa after a big battle on the eastern slope of Omabi (known today as Goat Mountain). "We sent them home crying," he'd say with a blustering laugh, as he praised the Nɨm, who returned safely into the isolation of the high Sierra Nevada meadows, herding many horses they took from the Wowa.

Battles between tribes or fights between individuals were never intended to purposely kill people, Grandpa stressed. Advance and retreat, tease and taunt, humiliate the enemy, he counseled. Killing was seldom necessary. Rather, he said, to touch one's enemy, to play with him and shame him, was to gain honor and esteem from one's peers. If you have to fight, he said, do so only in this way.

Cha:tiniu was my ancestors' home for eons past. From season to season they lived in the same way, until one day strangers appeared.

CHAPTER THREE

THE FIRST STRANGERS

One day a long time ago, an Indian who probably escaped from one of the Spanish missions near the central California coast visited Kana´au and Cha:tiniu. Grandma said he warned our family to hide. "People on horses are coming to get you," he said. "I just ran away from their church." But the horsemen never appeared. Grandma said one of her Mamas, as she described her aunts and great-aunts, had told her the story when she was a young girl.

Indians from other tribes occasionally visited Cha:tiniu, sharing stories about strangers they met on the trails, men different from any they had ever seen before. Their skin was very light, and their bodies were completely covered with clothing. Ever so slowly these strangers began a chain of events that changed my family's world.

In the late 1700s explorers forged northward from colonized Mexico seeking new locales at which to build their missions; several expeditions entered the San Joaquin Valley during Spain's control of California between 1776 and 1826. Although no missions were established in the valley, in northern California whole villages were relocated to Franciscan missions along the coastline of the Pacific Ocean.

José Joaquin Moraga guided the earliest known expedition. It left Monterey in September 1776, traveling three days up a river later to be named the San Joaquin. After fording the river (in what later became Fresno County), the expedition traveled eastward another day's journey before retracing its route. The Spaniards didn't enter the mountains to their east.

Grandpa spoke of strangers seen by his father's great-grandfather on the old Indian trail that crosses the San Joaquin River near today's Kerckhoff Dam. This might have been the Spanish expedition led by Moraga's son, Lt. Gabriel Moraga, who left Mission San Juan Bautista in September 1806. After entering the San Joaquin Valley, this expedition marched eastward along the San Joaquin River and eventually camped near today's Millerton Lake. "Farther in the interior of the mountains," wrote the expedition's priest, Fray Pedro Muñoz, on October 13, "on the bank of the river they descried a village called Pizcache of about 200 souls, with a chief named 'Sujoyucomu.'" Sujoyucomu told Moraga that twenty years earlier his village was visited by soldiers from the other side of the mountains who Moraga assumed were from New Mexico.[1] There was a fight during that earlier visit, Sujoyucomu said, during which many Indians were killed. Pizcache may have been located about where the town of Auberry is today.

Following a major drought in the 1830s that destroyed planted grain crops and the natural forage necessary to feed farm animals that had been introduced to Alta California by the Spanish, the Mexican government ordered the Mexican landowners to kill all their horses to ensure the cattle's survival. Instead the landowners drove their herds into the San Joaquin Valley for temporary haven, where they multiplied rapidly. (Thousands of mustangs were a common sight in the early 1850s, when miners entered this valley in search of gold.)

Grandpa said that before the early 1800s the men in our family occasionally left Cha:tiniu, walking westward toward the Komotini on one of their periodic raids. Women were a valuable trade item, so they stole some to trade with the sibitɨ Nɨm. When they discovered horses in the Komotini's territory, they stole them, too, for food. But as they watched the Mexicans ride the horses, Grandpa said our ancestors had a great idea. Instead of eating them, the men learned to break and ride them, and soon, in addition to women, they stole horses, who were more valuable in their trading expeditions.

Grandpa was quick to explain that the taking of women wasn't stealing in the modern sense of the word. The Komotini were our enemies, he said, and to take something from an enemy required great skill and courage. We were to have courage when dealing with our enemies but were never to steal from friends, or from strangers who were not our enemies.

José Castro was commandant-general of California during the 1842–45 administration of Gov. Manuel Micheltorena. At the foot of the Sierra Nevada, where the San Joaquin River flows into the San Joaquin Valley, Castro established a military outpost in the early 1840s, near where Friant is today.

After Gov. Pio Pico awarded Castro a 47,740-acre land grant on April 4, 1846, which extended westward from near Friant along both sides of the San Joaquin River, Castro built a house near the outpost. Except for occasional horse raids by Indians, the vaqueros who tended Castro's horses and four hundred head of cattle had a pretty good life.

Grandpa shared a story he heard from his grandpa, who was also named Sakɨma, describing how the whole family sometimes walked to Friant to steal horses in the mid-1800s, probably from Castro's rancho. "The *punyonas* [Mexicans] came in and raised hell with us. They chased us up the river as we herded their horses before us. We [the family] always managed to escape," he smiled. (After the Mexican-American War, in which Castro played a major role on behalf of the Mexican government, his land claim was rejected by the U.S. Land Commission, and the rancho became public domain under U.S. law.)

Horses drastically changed how my ancestors traveled, shortening their journeys over the Sierras to visit friends on the eastern side or to hot springs at several places in the Sierras. The family began to ride to hot springs south of Cha:tiniu, known today as Mono Hot Springs, and even the horses soaked in the recuperative water.

Early in this century, after his parents moved to Peyakinu, west of today's Redinger Lake, Grandpa said they and others pastured their horses in winter at Kawaiya, which means "where horses are kept," the Long Ridge of today. "The Chukchansi used to come over and steal horses from there," he said.

Other Nɨm had different experiences with the first strangers. "The Indians were down near Pollasky [Friant] on the San Joaquin River, getting the roots for their baskets," reminisced Nellie Turner Williams.[2] Soldiers appeared, made camp, and after cooking tortillas, brought tortillas and flour to "some of the old Indian ladies." Most of the women were afraid of being poisoned, so they dumped the flour on the ground and hid themselves. One brave woman exclaimed, "Oh, they look like they're trying to be friendly. . . . I'll eat it and if I die, well, okay." She didn't die, and after the soldiers left, all the women tasted the tortilla, which the first woman said tasted "pretty good." They also scooped up some of the flour from the ground for future use.

Contact between Indians and Mexicans wasn't always friendly. Mrs. Williams recalled another story about when a group of Indians saw some Spaniards dressed in white clothes. One of them, probably a priest, was on his knees and appeared to be praying. "He sounded like a 'bull.'"[3] The Indians killed all of them.

Deadly disease was rampant in the early 1830s. An epidemic, of either cholera or malaria, raged unchecked throughout the central San Joaquin Valley, killing hundreds of Indians during one season. Although my grandparents had no personal knowledge of these epidemics, they knew of deadly illnesses during their great-grandparents' generation which were suffered by other mountain tribes. Chief Tenaya claimed that a large tribe, probably the Ahwaneechee who lived in the Yosemite Valley before Tenaya moved there in the 1840s with his followers, was nearly destroyed when they were attacked by a fatal "black sickness."[4] (Grandma said buckwheat heals malaria.) The Spaniards and Mexicans also shared two other unwelcome diseases: smallpox, which was always deadly, and syphilis, which usually left its mark.

Grandpa enjoyed telling one story over and over again, about his journey across the mountains, when he followed in the footsteps of his grandpa, Sakɨma. He described the trails and landmarks where he'd stop to rest or camp. Several years after Grandpa's death, I, too, began walking in my ancestors' footsteps. My first trek began at a little-known trail Grandpa described which began not far from Cha:tiniu, near today's Mammoth Pool dam.

It was summer. The heat of the morning sun beat on our backs as I, a cousin, Richard Lavell, a Nɨm boy, Bill Johnson, and a non-Indian friend, Donn Lusby, who is a professional photographer, walked up the mountainside. The steep climb reminded me of my ancestors' perseverance as they walked or rode where I now did.

Since Grandpa said he'd stopped at both places, we rested at campsites near thirst-quenching springs in today's Sample Meadow and near the hot pools that offered a warm, nourishing bath at Mono Hot Springs. At each camp I shared some of Grandpa's stories about the past. In the dark coolness of early evening, beneath a brilliant full moon enhanced by bright light from a warm fire, I sang and danced as Grandpa and Grandma taught me. Then Bill thrilled all of us as he performed intertribal powwow dances he'd learned for modern competitions.

We walked on the next day, crossing the San Joaquin River where it's now dammed by Florence Lake, walking higher and higher until we were above 11,000 feet, above the trees and in the steep granite crevasse of Piute Pass. Suddenly I heard a thundering noise. Turning, I saw men astride horses coming toward me, whipping their mounts over the trail. I recognized Grandpa immediately, dressed in Levis and cowboy shirt, his high-topped boots

Left to right: Richard Lavell, Donn Lusby, Bill Johnson, and Gaylen Lee in 1993, at Piute Pass in the central Sierra Nevada. (Courtesy of Donn Lusby)

snug in the stirrups as he rode his saddled mount. There were others I didn't know, riding bareback, dressed only in loincloths, their hair dancing in the breeze. Intuitively, I knew they were my ancestors, great-grandpas and their grandpas, their destination the lakes that dotted the distant landscape, onward and downward to camp with their friends, to trade women or captured Spanish and Mexican horses for obsidian, pine nuts, or whatever curiosity they fancied. Grandpa smiled at me as he rode past, and I felt his touch as I walked on.

Phew! Filthy, stinking, uncouth strangers traveled across the virgin west, leaving behind a litany of *chakwashib,* meaning "part-white children," at Indian settlements across the frontier. They walked or rode into the land of the Nɨm. They are heroes of the American West. They began the invasion of our land.

Around the turn of this century, "Indian Frank" recalled "old man *Chepo.* . . . Once little boy, long time ago, [saw] white man come, kill big bear, catch beaver in trap. Go away."[5] The white man was probably one of the early trappers who occasionally entered the central Sierra Nevada in the 1800s.

Yankees actually began to visit California during the Spanish occupation of the late 1700s, initially journeying in sea vessels, the only route westward. They sailed thousands of miles southward from Boston Harbor, circled Cape Horn, and then sailed north thousands of miles more to the coastal port of Monterey in Alta California. Their quest was the sea otter, for whom they searched up and down the Pacific Coast.

After Meriwether Lewis and William Clark glowingly described the wide variety of furbearing animals they had seen during their overland journey to the Pacific Northwest in 1804–6, fur trappers ventured west by foot and on horseback, fanning out in small overland expeditions from the largely unsettled American frontier. Occasionally, they fought Indian tribes; occasionally, they "married" Indian women.

Sierra Nevada trails beckoned some of these men, whose descriptions kindled in others a quest to explore, a quest that eventually changed even more my ancestors' lives. Jedediah Smith (in 1826) and Ewing Young (in 1832) were trappers who explored the San Joaquin River drainage as they hunted northward from Los Angeles, after their overland journeys on the Old Spanish Trail from Santa Fe, New Mexico.

Prodded by the financial depression of 1837, many eastern and north-central settlers sought new homes in the still largely uncharted west, journeying by covered wagon, on horseback, or by foot toward Texas or Oregon. The federal government's doctrine of Manifest Destiny, which preached the Americans' right to inhabit and govern the continent from coast to coast, with no regard for the native inhabitants, justified this aggressive plunge westward. In November 1841 the Bartleson-Bidwell party, the first organized overland emigrant train to travel west, arrived in northern California; within a week another party of emigrants reached southern California. The American overland migration had begun.

Also in the 1840s the U.S. Topographical Bureau ordered Col. John Charles Fremont to explore the west; his several expeditions were sanctioned by the Department of War. Fremont's reconnaissance was intended to record the rivers, mountains, and terrain. But he and his father-in-law, Sen. Thomas H. Benton of Missouri, whose influence enabled Fremont's expeditions, hoped to open the previously uncharted west to settlement.

"Indians were still around the camp at night," Fremont noted in his diary in December 1845, during his third expedition to California.[6] They had entered the Sierras, following the Kings River eastward. "I found the mountain extremely rocky in the upper parts, the streams break through canons, but wooded up to the granite ridges which compose its rocky eminences," Fremont wrote. After descending the high peaks, the expedition camped at the headwaters of the San Joaquin River, close to Cha:tiniu. "During the night the Indians succeeded in killing one of our best mules. . . . An Indian had driven an arrow nearly through his body. . . . [As the expedition descended through the forests] we chose a different way . . . but it was rocky and rough everywhere. . . . The chasms through which the rivers roared were dark against the snow." It is unclear from Fremont's account whether their return route was back down the Kings River or along the San Joaquin River. In either case, the Indians, who were undoubtedly after their horses for food, were probably Nɨm.

The sands of time whirled around my ancestors as the explorations of Spanish, Mexican, and American adventurers touched their lives. Only dusty memories survive. A new storm would soon envelop them, leaving in its wake destruction and chaos.

CHAPTER FOUR

WHEN EVERYTHING TURNS GREEN

Up high I fly where it is cold.
I go north in April where it is cool.
When the rain and snow hit my bald head
I go south where it is warm.
                    Buzzard's song, as told by Grandma

My family was aware of four cyclical seasons in the old days, but neither days nor weeks nor months nor years were measured. Day began at dawn and ended with darkness. Animals and birds, trees and plants, announced the seasons. The family listened to and watched everything, for everything spoke to them: the land, the sky, the wind, the rain, the snow; the plants, the birds, the insects, the animals. Their lives flowed with the seasons. Each was a friend revealing when to move to the cool air of the mountains or return to the warmer climate; when to hunt and gather, to hold ceremonies, to build the winter camp, to gather materials for basket making.

My ancestors watched and listened. After the long, cold days of winter, when the ground disappeared beneath a deep cover of snow and fog darkened the sky as it lifted occasionally from the great valley below into the mountains, the *bohenab,* meaning "leader," was alerted. Perhaps he heard coyote pups yapping in the distance or saw a swath of green grass in the melting snow. He might have looked into the night sky and saw the return of *ewaniwɨ,* meaning "walking all together," what we know today as the Milky Way. Any of these signs could tell him that it was *puhiduwa,* meaning "when everything turns green," Grandma said, the season we know today as spring.

The bohenab would send his *natɨnab,* meaning "runner" or "messenger," from settlement to settlement to announce the annual renewal ceremony: over the ridges to the Wowa or across the San Joaquin River to the unapatɨ Nɨm. This ceremony was always held in early spring, at a large meadow in the mountains, Grandma said. It was the first of many *ogi,* meaning "big time," celebrations held throughout spring, summer, and fall when feasting, playing, visiting, and dancing prevailed. I was about nine years old when Grandma described these gatherings. That's how my family's children were taught: a parent or grandparent, an aunt or uncle, decided it was time to teach something. Perhaps we were eating or out walking; for no reason obvious to me, Grandma or Grandpa were impelled to share something they decided it was time to learn.

Grandma said that before the renewal ceremony began the bohenab would capture a young *kwi´na,* a golden eagle. "Kwi´na is strong and pure," she said. "Wiwison [Bald Eagle] is lazy." Kwi´na was kept caged, but he was well cared for, raised by hand and fed rabbits, squirrels, salmon, and other creatures he would normally hunt in the wild. His presence was important to the ceremonies' success, and his feathers were carefully plucked for ceremonial or personal use.

Despite her advanced age Grandma vividly recalled her childhood, when she watched Kwi´na dance at Cha:tiniu. Kwi´na was held by a dancer from the Eagle side, she said, who was joined by other people, all of whom wore capes and headbands fashioned from eagle feathers, their arms also banded with Kwi´na's feathers.

Everyone moved like Kwi´na, their arms like wings, swaying and flying, swaying and flying, swaying and flying. Suddenly Grandma took my hand, and we danced together as others had done scores of years before.

At the end of the renewal ceremony the Wowa were offered a chance to "buy" Kwi´na, Grandma said. They usually did, paying with horses, baskets, or beads. If the Wowa declined, Kwi´na was offered to other Indians.

The Nɨm no longer gather during puhiduwa for the renewal ceremony. Early in this century a bohenab begrudgingly stopped the ceremony, Grandma said, because of the pressure and chastisement from white people as well as ministers of the Christian church. They believed our ceremonies were "pagan" and "wicked." Kwi´na still flies though. A few Nɨm know his dance, and although Kwi´na is no longer captured, when we are able to obtain his feathers, they are protected and cared for.

The land is changed as the twentieth century draws to a close. The physical appearance of my family's old-time lifestyle—their homes, encampments, most of the old ways—the ogi, even Grandma and Grandpa, are gone. But within the bosom of my family much of their lifestyle survives.

Sometimes, when I'm out-of-doors, I sense someone. Peering skyward, I see Kwi´na soaring on wind currents, gliding easily, thrusting himself with great strength to unbelievable heights. My heart soars with him. Kwi´na, the mighty hunter and provider, "is over all of us," my grandparents said. They never described him as God or gods, the Great Spirit or any other spirit, to be worshipped or honored. Rather, they said, he is the finest example of the type of person we are taught to be. He is also our messenger, carrying our thoughts to the six directions: north, south, east, and west, up and down.

It began this way:

Many, many thousands of years ago, the whole earth was covered with water. Grebe, Turtle, and Muskrat were sitting on a log that was floating. They were sitting there for four days. They were wondering if they could reach the bottom. They decided to try, and one at a time they tried to swim to the bottom. Turtle went first. He held his breath and dove into the water. Down, down, down he went, but his air did not last as long as he thought it would. He had to return to the surface. He was gasping for air when he reached the top. Muskrat decided to try to reach the bottom, so he tried. He took air into his lungs and down into the water he went. He went a little farther than Turtle, but his lungs were burning so he returned to the surface. His air had run out and he died on the way back to the top. He had drowned and it took him two days to reach the top. This is why Muskrat only lives in shallow water. Grebe dove, and it took her two and one-half days to reach bottom. She got to the bottom and picked up a handful of mud. She started to swim back to the surface. On her way back up the water washed the mud out of her hand. When she reached the top she passed out from exhaustion. Turtle pulled Grebe onto the log. He looked into her hand and only found a grain of sand. It had gotten caught under her claw. Turtle picked the sand out of her claw and threw it. Where it hit the water and skipped, it made land. The land was soft and muddy. Eagle, who had called these three, was flying overhead. He was seeing the work the three had done. He was getting tired. He kept getting lower and lower. His wings touched the mud and wherever he touched, he made mountains.

—as told by Grandpa

As do most children who are given guns, I hunted birds and small animals. Grandma cautioned me, however, never to shoot at Kwiʹna, because of his great importance. I had a lesson to learn. One day I shot at Kwiʹna, and although I missed, the enormity of what I had done overwhelmed me. I didn't dare tell Grandma, but after I became sick, I mean really sick, Mom questioned me. She scolded me fiercely when I told her I'd shot at Kwiʹna. "You never shoot your pet," she exclaimed. (I'll explain the relationship of *pet* to our word *puk* in a bit.)

Kwi´na is leader of my family's *nakweti*, meaning "side" in our language. It was anthropologists in the early 1900s who introduced the word *moiety* (which comes from the French word for *half*). Many Nɨm have stopped using the traditional word nakweti, saying instead *clan* (which is defined as a common interest or characteristic). My grandparents never changed. They clung to the old way of describing the two sides as Kwi´na and Isha, Eagle and Coyote. Grandma and my Grandpa Willie said there were only these two sides, each led by its own bohenab.

The historical leadership of the Eagle side was inherited by the Pomona family generations past, as far back at least as my great-great-great-grandfather, Panau. Before American settlement began, he lived southwest of today's Fish Creek Mountain, at a place called Panau, meaning "grass seed place." Panau's son, my great-great-grandfather, Pimono, inherited the leadership when his father died.

Pimono's son, also named Panau, was my great-grandfather. He was born about 1862. Years later, after American settlement was well under way, he was also known as Dick Pimono. After his first and second wives failed to give birth to an heir, he took his third wife, Saiyu, who gave him four children.

For some unknown reason, perhaps Saiyu's death, Panau then married Hiwaiyuni, my great-grandmother. Hiwaiyuni, who was also known as Kitty, was born in about 1878. In those pretransition days she, too, was a bohenab, through inheritance from her father, Honitiwit.

Mom remembers her grandfather, Panau. "I was a little girl when he took me to town [from his home near Fish Creek Mountain] in a horse-drawn buggy. He bought me high-topped shoes, the kind you needed a needle to lace them up through the holes."

After Panau died his and Hiwaiyuni's son, Tunani, inherited the leadership of the Eagle side. Tunani, whose English name is Willie Pomona (a corruption of Pimono), was born about 1898. He was bohenab of the Eagle side when he died in 1987. Willie Pomona is

Mom's father and my grandfather. His family continues the leadership tradition.

The bohenab of the Coyote side has been inherited through the Sherman family, and is now Frank Sherman. Grandpa Willie's sisters, Lizzie and Nancy, were married to Frank Sherman's brothers, Leo and Johnnie.

Leaders were ordinary, family-oriented people. Grandpa Willie married twice. First he married my grandmother, Emma Moore, whose Nɨm name is Mahaunai. They had two children: Aunt Ethel, who was named Omo´kadi, and Mom, who was named Hiwaiyuni. Grandma Emma died in 1931. Many years later Grandpa Willie and Julia Riley had three children: Jeannie, Catherine, and Harry, who, when he was named Panau, continued the family tradition. Grandpa Willie lived at Saksakaniu, northeast of Fish Creek Mountain. The property is still owned by his heirs.

In the old days the bohenab was identifiable at special gatherings by the headdress of Kwi´na's feathers he wore. The last time Grandma saw a bohenab wearing this headdress was in the early 1920s. She didn't know why the custom ended, but probably the inroads of a prejudiced culture doomed the display. Once, my grandparents said, the bohenab also wore a halo made with Kwi´na's feathers, but that custom ended before they were born.

The bohenab does not dictate decisions for the people, Grandma said. Rather he seeks guidance from others, especially the older people. That is why we call him a leader, not a chief, whose position permits him to make decisions. To help me understand the bohenab's position in relation to the people, Grandma and Grandpa Willie used the expression kobewɨnɨdɨ, meaning "stands in front." Among other things, not so long ago the bohenab led ceremonies, settled disputes, and guided the decisions for his side. The bohenab (and also the medicine people) was expected to act humbly at all times to properly serve everyone. Unfortunately, as the older people, who were raised in the Nɨm traditions, have died, the bohenab's role has diminished.

Front row, left to right: Mike Lee and Jacquie Lee. *Back row, left to right:* Ruby Pomona, Willie Pomona, and Gaylen Lee. The family was in Yosemite National Park in the mid-1970s attending the annual Indian Days festival. (Courtesy of Ethel Temple)

Each side also had one or more natinab to assist the bohenab, and who were sent by him to all the settlements of both sides to announce dance ceremonies, mourning ceremonies, or an acorn feed. The natinab carried the news.

My grandparents stressed the people's expectation of the bohenab's exemplification of Kwi´na, whom he represented. He has to be strong, physically and in character. He must soar above the mundane aspects of life. He must be alert and always aware of everything going on around him. He must be available to his people at any time.

Grandma said, "We have always been here," originally as "animal people," who had wisdom and intelligence, and later as wise and intelligent "human people." The only difference between the two was physical form and the "human people's" ability to care for all things.

My grandparents taught that humans can communicate with all life and that we should never attempt to dominate anything. All forms of life are our "little brothers." Even the tiny, flitting hummingbird, Grandpa said, was of great value. "He talked for Kwi´na when we were still animal people. He was Eagle's nat+nab." This meaningful identity with and brotherhood to all living things centers our lives and permeates all of our activity, they said, likening this idea to "caring and sharing."

Our language has no words to describe religion, church, or spiritual activities. No structure or organization was necessary in the old days to care for and share with anyone. How we lived our daily lives naturally manifested caring and sharing. Our ceremonies were always performed out-of-doors and within view of the animals and birds, the land and sky, all of life. My grandparents said there was no separation between the material, that which is apparent, and what non-Indians call the spiritual, that which they believe is invisible. They are one.

Non-Indians ask so many questions! If only they'd be still for a while, they'd learn: from the wind and fog, from the heat of the day, from the darkness of the night; by watching the insects, birds, animals, and reptiles. They all have knowledge to share with us, my grandparents said.

Each day, when we awaken, Grandma said we should say "Thank you," but not to any specific person or thing. "Thank you" embraces the seen and unseen world, centering us for the day, for the things we'll do, for the people we'll meet. It's not the form of prayer as taught by other cultures. It's simply "Thank you."

Ohob doesn't translate easily into English. The best translation my grandparents could come up with was to describe ohob as "strength"; it is energy, it is alive, they said. Depending on a specific need, for instance, if the need is to run fast in a sporting event speak to the ohob, the strength, of Kwi´na, who is identified with swift flight. Kwi´na's ohob strengthens us. If the air needs cleansing, speak to the ohob of the wind, and the wind will blow away the bad air. Whatever the human need is, there is an ohob—of an animal, bird, reptile, insect, plant, or tree, of any life-form or life-giving element—to help us.

My grandparents also explained how to identify one's *puk*. A puk can be an animal, bird, seed, tree, rock, flower, whatever it is that comes to a person at a specific time of life. It is the "who and what" of a person's being. Grandma said that in the old days each person learned his puk's identity through dreams or from its repeated appearance in everyday life. The ohob of each person's puk is always available.

After white people came years ago, Grandma said, because they didn't understand what the Nɨm meant when they said *puk,* someone apparently decided, "Oh, you mean like a pet." Probably, she added with exasperation, the Nɨm agreed. Even today some people, when referring to their puk in conversation, use the word *pet,* but not intending a dog or a cat.

My grandparents said the word *sacred* does not belong in our language because there are no sacred places or things. They described powerful places, perhaps where a bohenab lived or where ogi or other special gatherings were held. These places were not sacred in the accepted definition of the word, that is, worthy of religious veneration and requiring specific protection. Actually, Grandma said, powerful places have their own way of protecting themselves, needing no help from anyone.

The ability to heal was a natural function of life. If an individual's puk was exceptionally strong, he or she could evolve naturally into a healer.

"Kus kwasaga lives high in the mountains," Grandma said. He has the power to heal the sick. For instance, Kus kwasaga is called if a child has a stomachache; the child's stomach is rubbed and Kus kwasaga's song is sung: "Sabu sabu sabu, kita kita kita. Ko to niya we, ko to niya we, pabohi ko to niya we," Grandma said. "Kus kwasaga's hands have suction cups on his fingers. He sucks out all the pain." If I become ill with an occasional stomachache, I still feel Grandma's healing hands and hear her sing "kita kita."

In the old days Grandma would have been identified as a *chauki-maidɨ,* meaning "one who makes well," an Indian doctor. Sometimes other people came to her for physical healing, but she ministered primarily to her own family.

A chaukɨmaidɨ knows if an illness is caused physically by injury or contagion, or by emotional distress. Each illness is treated distinctly and differently. Grandma used medicinal plants to heal, as did her dad, Jim Moore, and she taught other family members to do the same. An individual must be chosen and taught by a chaukɨ-maidɨ, Grandma said. He or she can't just decide to be one.

I cherish the times we gathered plants, when Grandma would explain a specific plant for a specific illness. She said she never experimented with plants, nor did her dad. "The plants told us what to use," she explained. But sometimes, Grandma said, all that is needed to heal illness is to "chase it away," by invoking a simple and direct order to the illness to leave.

Not all chaukɨmaidɨ heal with plants. Some, but not Grandma, suck illness from their patient's body with a *to'ish.* She described the to'ish as a tubular pipe, made from either a hollowed-out piece of branch from the mountain mahogany plant or, less often, from clay soil formed into a tube, hollowed out with a stick, air-dried for several hours and then fired for several more hours. Some chaukɨ-maidɨ used both pipes. They also heal by shaking a cocoon rattle to mark the beat as they sing healing songs. Grandma gave me her rattle before she died.

Pauwɨha, who lives in certain springs and rivers, can also cause illness, Grandma said. Pauwɨha has long, very shiny hair, sometimes blond, sometimes black, but it is never seen, because it jumps back into the spring when someone approaches, Grandma said. If, by chance, Pauwɨha is glimpsed, only its hair and body are seen, never its face. If the face is seen, Grandma said, the person becomes "sick, many different ways."

Dreams are a powerful source of information, Grandma said, and should be listened to. She said some people use the datura plant to guide dreams, and she described its preparation and effect. Like Grandma, I don't discuss datura, because, unlike in the old days when the plant was respected, some people are now using drugs improperly, and if datura is ingested in the wrong way it can cause a person to die.

Grandma was often asked to heal ghost dreams. She knew special songs that chased away the ghosts of dead people who wanted to remain in this world but would disturb the living if they did. Ghosts are also chased away by washing with *kwusidap,* the wormwood plant, or, as Grandpa suggested, by hanging kwusidap outside the house. Ghosts would also leave, he said, if a wing from the bluejay or woodpecker was attached to a very small bow and hung outside.

Some healers, but not Grandma, also use *sog,* wild tobacco, to chase away ghosts. It is gathered, dried, and crushed, then stored until needed, she said. To create the healing smoke sog is put into a pipe and lit. The smoke is first inhaled, then exhaled, chasing away the ghosts. Store-bought pipes replaced hand-fashioned ones after they were introduced by the white man.

Ghosts stink and are hot. When Mom was a teenager in the 1940s, she recalls returning home after the family had walked to and from North Fork to go to the movie theater. She says her Grandpa, Jim Moore, who had stayed home, inquired if they had seen "the ghost down the road." "We hadn't and told him so." He told them it smelled really bad and its presence created heat.

Life has its opposites: good and bad, night and day, yes and no. There are opposites in healing, too. A *puhagei* is the opposite of a chaukimaidi. A puhagei hurts people with "bad" medicine rather than healing them, Grandma said.

When Gloria and I were growing up we were often warned by our grandparents to act in such a way that a puhagei could not harm us. For instance, when we walked on a trail we never peed there but went into the bushes so a puhagei wouldn't find the sign and use it to hurt us. We were also told not to eat food served by strangers or by people mistrusted by our family.

Grandma said a puhagei's medicine was usually rattlesnake poison. We were not, however, at the mercy of a puhagei but were taught how to protect ourselves with mental resistance. We are not a fearful family, but we are taught to be alert to everything that goes on around us. Grandma said that's "using your head."

In the early twentieth century, after an unusual number of people died here from poisoning, the Paiute Indians living east of the Sierra Nevada near Bishop and Lone Pine started calling the Nɨm nɨmadɨka, meaning "people who eat each other," because, then, there was so much poisoning going on. Grandma said the puhagei's actions increased about that time because they thought the bohenab's duties had been squelched.

When she was a young girl Grandma heard about a mental duel between two people who lived near North Fork; one of them was killed solely by the focused mental strength of the other. Years ago, she added, strong medicine people actually had contests in which one would attempt to kill the other with thoughts.

A chaukɨmaidɨ can also change what appears to be real to what is actually real, Grandma said. Weather can be changed, if it's necessary. I watched Grandma ask the rain to rain and the snow to snow. They always responded. She said she was successful because people born in summer, as she was, are "good at making it rain because they want to cool down." She could also, by the simple act of asking, bring back the sunshine after the storm. She always cautioned: never demand change. "You always ask. And don't forget to say 'thank you' afterward."

Sometimes, when I'm standing outside and the wind is blowing fiercely while the fog swirls around me, I hear Grandpa say, "The wind's fighting the fog." I'll sing his personal song to the wind, the fog goes away, the sun shines again. Grandma sometimes burned pine pitch to "chase away the fog."

The journey of a *tïbipahabich,* a tarantula, predicts rain. Grandpa said if you see a tïbipahabich walking uphill it knows rain is coming and is getting out of the way. Sure enough, whenever I see a tïbipahabich walk uphill on a sunny day, soon afterward there is an unpredicted storm.

Each of the four directions is a powerful aid in healing, Grandpa said. He described four primary colors: yellow represents the rising sun in the east; red, the heat of the day in the south; blue, the coolness of the western sky; and white, the purity of the northern snow. These colors were once used for body paint during ceremonies, and appear throughout our territory in images and designs painted with earth pigments on large boulders or in rock shelters. "Don't go near there [the paintings]," Grandma warned, "because they're places of power." Whether hunting or hiking, I avoid them.

Our ceremonial beadwork, too, reflects the colors of the four directions. After glass beads were introduced to California's Indians by traders, the Nïm replaced shell beads with glass. Likewise, after yarn was introduced by pioneer settlers, belts formerly woven with milkweed, worn by singers at special gatherings, were woven with yellow, red, blue, and white yarn. Some ladies continue to weave yarn belts in a variety of colors for garment decoration.

In the old days the bright rays of the rising sun awakened sleeping families in their snug houses, piercing the interior darkness through east-facing doorways. Our family was taught not to fear darkness, but we know it's at night that Great Horned Owl is out and about. "If you hear this owl during the night, chase it away," Grandma said. He is an omen of death, singing the names of those who will die. Within a very short time, three people who are called by him die. He is an unwelcome visitor.

Grandma counseled, "If people live right, do good, think good thoughts, when death comes they will slip quietly away." "Don't be afraid to die," she added. Death is part of the full round of life: birth, life, death. She advised watching the old people, many of whom, knowing days beforehand that they're going to die, give to beloved family members their special personal belongings.

Our family continues to participate in the *ana yagan* ceremony. This ceremony of ritual singing and dancing is intended to help the deceased in his or her journey from this dimension into another. It's a time of mourning for the survivors, when tears flow freely. The ana yagan is a vital force. The dead don't want to leave but yearn to remain with family and friends. Since after death a person is, for a short while, a *choap,* a ghost, he can bother people with his presence. By singing and dancing, we help the dead complete their journey.

Newly arrived Christian missionaries early in this century viewed this ceremony of compassion and warmth as a pagan ritual. They damned the ana yagan as well as other ceremonies and successfully influenced the federal government to outlaw them. Because the bohenabs continued the ana yagan at isolated locales, away from the prying eyes and ears of white people, it has survived.

My earliest memory of an ana yagan is as a three-year-old, sleeping a lot, eating a little, occasionally playing with other children. By the time I was six, sleeping and eating were minimal. I was too busy playing tag with other kids. Mom and Grandma yelled at us when we made too much noise. Eventually I stopped playing around and began dancing, and, as the years passed, Grandma and Grandpa taught me many songs. When I was about thirty years old, Grandpa Willie asked me to sing with him. He taught me many of his songs. My grandparents would be happy to see children today joining in the ritual dancing and singing quietly along with the singers. It is good that the ana yagan ceremony remains strong; it's needed.

Unfortunately the pressure of a faster-paced life has resulted in adaptation to the white man's ways. The ana yagan has changed. In the old days a four-night ceremony was led by the bohenab and singers of the side opposite to the deceased. Now the ceremony is usually two nights, and usually the singers are people from both sides.

Once the women of the deceased's family embalmed the body with specific plant material to prevent its putrefaction during the mourning ceremony, and the immediate family avoided eating salt so the body wouldn't swell. Professional morticians embalm the body now. Then, after the body was dressed in its finest clothing, it was kept in the house for viewing. Old women sang and danced around the body; the deceased's family walked over the body. This is called the *yaga niga*. Some families still bring the body home for viewing before burial, and occasionally the singers sing and dance by the coffin. But most often the body remains at the funeral home for viewing, until burial.

The ana yagan is now usually held on two alternate nights with burial in between. After it becomes dark, singers position themselves on the sidelines as a designated person leads the dancers, one by one, in a circular ritual dance around a large fire that is kept burning throughout the night. This dance is called *aha´na*.

Imagine the ancient melodies piercing the darkness; the structured cadence of thumping feet on hard ground and the occasional strong expelling of breath from individual dancers propelling them around and around the circle, beginning at nightfall. The people rest only for a bit, then begin again, continuing until dawn. When many mourners dance together around a fire, as when Grandpa Willie died in 1987, and there is no sound or light except that of the crackling, burning wood and the night sky ablaze with twinkling light, footfall unites with footfall and the surge of energy builds and builds, propelling the deceased into another dimension.

On the second night of dancing, as the sun rises in the eastern sky, as tears flow freely, each mourner selects and throws a bundle of the deceased's clothing into the fire, over and over again until nothing is left to burn. This is another way to keep the choap away, and also aids the grieving relatives by eliminating material evidence of their loved one.

Interment in a cemetery is now common. I sometimes still see an old woman approach the grave, grieving visibly. One of Grandpa Willie's kinfolk, Emma Chepo, did this the day we buried him. Her keening voice chanted an age-old song as other mourners, silent and respectful, watched. Then we lowered Grandpa Willie into his grave.

"Grandma Lizzie's father died while he was tracking deer over by Dandy's place [at Long Ridge above the San Joaquin River]," Grandpa John reminisced one day. "A snake bit him. They burned him on fire." In the old days, the body was the last thing put on the fire. Grandma said that long ago the ashes were scattered to feed the earth that in turn feeds all things. "Life is always a circle," she added.

Cremation is seldom practiced anymore, and certainly not as it was done in the old days. Cremation ended with the influence of the Christian church and at about the same time that the federal government attempted to stop the ana yagan.

In a final act of cleansing, following the burning and as the fire slows in intensity, beginning with the closest family members and ending with the last friend, each person's face is washed with kwusidap, the wormwood plant, soaked in hot water. Everyone then gathers to eat breakfast, to reminisce, to shed a few more tears, and finally departs.

In the old days baskets were collected from people on the side opposite to the deceased to be given as gifts to the family at the end of the ana yagan. Money is collected today.

Years ago the women in the deceased's immediate family cut their hair into a very short bob immediately after their faces were washed and then smeared their faces with ash from the fire. Grandma called this act *sikina*, a word seldom heard anymore as the practice has virtually disappeared. Day after day the family cried in grief, their tears streaking their unwashed faces. They remained in their homes for two years. Some families now mourn for only one year because of the need to pursue modern employment.

To come out of mourning, there is a final ceremony called *tiwak-wai*. People dance for one night, and at dawn in a final cleansing, the mourners have their faces washed with kwusidap.

Grandma recalled attending a ceremony years ago which resembled the cremation that occurred in her childhood. On a night chosen by the bohenab, family members of all the people who had died the previous year brought effigies dressed in clothing that was held back from the original mourning ceremony. The effigies were burned in the ceremonial fire in imitation of the original ana yagan. Grandma said this ceremony developed after cremation and the ana yagan were banned and before the bohenab resumed the ceremony in secret. This ceremony, too, has disappeared.

Neither Grandma, nor Grandpa, nor Grandpa Willie knew anything about the non-Indian concept of reincarnation. Even so, they said, following death we remain here as animal people, as we were long ago. If a person is strong and has power, such as a leader or a healer, they said that person can choose the animal, insect, reptile, bird, or whatever, they want to be after death. Often one chose his puk. While driving out of a canyon on a steep dirt road one day, I saw a very large rattlesnake moving slowly across the road in front of me. I stopped and waited for him to pass, not wanting to hurt him, as I didn't know whose relative he was. Before they died, Grandma and Grandpa told me who they would be after death. We saw Grandma within a few days after she died, just as she said, a creature we had not seen here before. She returns each year. Grandpa, too, appeared, as he said he would.

My grandparents never spoke of a spirit world. There was only now, life continuing in different form. Although they had heard about the white man's heaven and hell, that concept belonged solely to the alien culture. Grandma assured me that there is a good life after death.

In the recent past many Nïm began calling the ana yagan a powwow, a word not of our language but originating in the American plains, where Indians gathered to dance, feast, and play games.

Powwows have been held for centuries in the midwestern United States. Probably when an English translation of the ana yagan was necessary in the early 1900s, a non-Indian chose powwow as the best description. Unfortunately many uninformed non-Indians assume an ana yagan is similar to the modern powwow, which includes competitive dancing and sales of Indian crafts. Some Nɨm prefer to describe the ana yagan as a cry ceremony or a mourning ceremony.

I don't fear that our culture will disappear, as many non-Indians suggest. The old people await us, as animal people, and life continues.

CHAPTER FIVE

SPRING, WHEN UNINVITED GUESTS BRING GIFTS OF DEATH

It's long ago, at the time called puhiduwa, the season now known as spring. The days are warmer; the world turns green as emerging grass blankets the earth and leaves reappear on the oaks. As darkness disappears into light, the song of young coyotes is heard. Heavy snow covers the mountains surrounding Cha:tiniu; rain falls occasionally on the tonobi at the meadow's edge. The air is brisk. The renewal ceremony has been held. Kwi´na has danced.

I can see my great-great-great-grandmother Chinitit out-of-doors with other women, weaving baskets, repairing or making clothing, cooking, watching children, gossiping, visiting. Men fish nearby streams, make bows and arrows, repair tools, gossip, and visit. Children play.

Scores of white men, gold miners mostly, strangers all, mounted and on foot, arrive at Cha:tiniu in the year 1851. Gunfire erupts, shattering the peaceful community; women and children disappear into the forest while the men stay behind to protect their families and homes. Then there is silence, except for the crackling sound of burning houses, granaries, sweathouses, shade arbors, and windbreaks. The white men burn everything.

History's version of what has become known as the Mariposa Indian War, which occurred over a few-month period in the spring of
1851, is well documented. The recollections of Indians and white
people sympathetic to their plight are hidden in isolated biogra-
phies and historical accounts.

Much has been written about the so-called Indian Wars in the
eastern United States that predate California's statehood by many
years. And about the Plains Indians' defense of their millions of acres
from the hordes of migrating settlers in the 1860s, 1870s, and 1880s,
ending with the massacre at Wounded Knee, South Dakota, in 1892,
forty years after miners first entered the central Sierra Nevada.

My tribe's resistance to the white man has been virtually ignored.
How we tried to live undisturbed as the American government attempted to destroy my family and others, culminating in the government's ultimate, deceitful misappropriation of our land.

Grandpa said all he knew about those times was what his own
grandfather had told him when he was a child: "Some of the old
people saw suntati [uniformed soldiers] at Cha:tiniu, long ago." It
is unlikely that more was ever said, in keeping with the family's
dictum that we not talk about "bad things." My grandparents cautioned not to discuss bad things or they could be "brought in" to
one's own experience. But it's time for the bad things that occurred
in the 1850s to be revealed, events that drastically changed Chinitit's life and her descendants' future.

History glorifies the first gold discovery by an American on January 24, 1848: James Wilson Marshall found yellow flecks in the
sand of the American River east of Sacramento, where he was con-
structing a sawmill. As if shot from a single giant cannon, thousands of men from every walk of life, from throughout the United
States and from other countries as well, exploded suddenly onto
the shores of the American and Sacramento rivers. They had one
purposeful thought: find gold and get rich. Their actions uninten-
tionally supported the federal government's quest for control of the

western United States by inundating California with Americans; within months, California was a state of the Union.

Logically, California's Indians were protected by the Hidalgo Treaty of 1848, signed at the conclusion of a war between the United States and Mexico, which guaranteed them the right to land and freedom from domination. Miners entering northern California, with their bad feelings toward the Indians they found living there, had other ideas.

As had occurred for more than two hundred years, since the English, French, and Dutch wrested the eastern seaboard from its native inhabitants, these newcomers shared a common attitude: annihilate the Indians, whose presence impeded the miners' search for gold. Indians were forced from their homes and often murdered; women and young girls were often raped. And the miners were amazed at the Indians' "strange conduct" when they occasionally retaliated against them.

Within a few months the initial gold fever lost its momentum. Some miners, impeded by the hordes of other men with similar determination and disgruntled when their fortunes were not discovered quickly, began to travel southward—by foot, on horseback, in wagons—to sift the sands in other rivers.

John Charles Fremont was ahead of them; he was one of the earliest arrivals in what became known as Mariposa County, where he purchased the Las Purisimas Land Grant. Fremont had returned to California after he was court-martialed for his involvement in the Mexican-American War. He initially sent his friend, Alexis Godey, who had accompanied him on some of his earlier explorations, and some Mexican miners to prospect the grant. After Godey discovered gold on a tributary of Agua Fria Creek, word of the new strike spread and other miners swarmed to the new strike. By December 1849, hundreds were in the vicinity.

Fremont developed a large estate at nearby Bear Valley. Today's travelers on Highway 49 pass through this quiet, pastoral valley a few miles north of the town of Mariposa, unaware of the excitement almost 150 years ago.

Luck had also visited a few miners in 1849. They found gold in the San Joaquin River near a place that later became known as Millerton. Within a year, a traveling French journalist, Etienne Derbec, found poor placers and evidence of mining that was apparently abandoned by disillusioned miners.

Still propelled by dreams of wealth, miners explored eastward into the Sierra Nevada, where they discovered productive strikes along the Merced and Chowchilla rivers and along the Fresno River, at places they named Coarsegold, today a thriving village on Highway 41 to Yosemite, and Grub Gulch, also on Highway 41 near today's town of Oakhurst. Little regard was given to the Indian people living there, our neighbors and sometimes enemies, the Wowa (the miners called them Chukchansi), who were swept into the maelstrom created by the gold-hungry miners.

Leading this invasion was James Savage, who arrived in Mariposa County in 1850. He was a controversial personality then, and still is. Some historians and biographers praise him as a military hero and a friend to the Indians. Others revile him. My family said Savage was a "bad man." His actions altered my ancestors' way of life. He cannot be ignored.

Savage was familiar with frontier life. He was born in 1823 in Illinois, then the western frontier. His family's legends suggest he may have lived with Plains Indians, either after he was kidnapped by them or after he ran away from home to live with them when he was a teenager. Savage was a small man but well built and physically strong. His skin was darkened by the sun, and he wore his brown hair long and tied below his shoulders.

Savage was twenty-three years old when he joined a wagon train heading west. After arriving in northern California he joined Fremont's California Battalion to fight Indians, and he also fought with Fremont against Mexican soldiers in the Mexican-American War. After gold was discovered, he worked for John Sutter.

Restless, Savage traveled south to Big Oak Flat, at the confluence of the Merced and Tuolomne rivers in Miwok Indian territory. He mined gold and opened a store to trade frontier necessaries to other miners and to Miwok who worked the river sand for him near his Big Oak Flat trading post. Disgruntled Indians destroyed the post within months of its opening, but some of its remains are visible today next to a souvenir store just outside the entrance to Yosemite Park on Highway 140.

Savage relocated again, opening a trading post where Agua Fria and Mariposa creeks meet, still in Miwok territory. A third post was opened next to the Fresno River, near where today's Madera County Road 415 crosses the river. He was now in Chukchansi territory.

Savage was shrewd. He quickly allied himself with the area's Indian tribes as their self-proclaimed friend. He also "married" young daughters of several Indian leaders, a common practice of European and American adventurers in the 1700s and 1800s who lived openly with Indian women on the American frontier. Robert Eccleston, a miner in the area, claimed that Savage had thirty-three "wives" between the ages of ten and twenty-two whom he dressed in white chemises with low necks and short sleeves and either red or blue skirts. "They are mostly low in stature & not unhandsome," Eccleston wrote in his diary. "They always look clean & sew neatly. [Savage] has a little house built for their accommodation."[1]

Savage continued to hire Indians to dig gold, paying them with trade goods, while he earned huge profits by underhandedly using a "Digger ounce" to measure the gold. ("Digger ounce" describes the method of using a lead slug to measure gold instead of the lighter, normal weight commonly used.) "One time . . . when a squaw came in and asked for some raisins," recalled Joseph Kinsman of a visit to the Fresno Crossing store, "Savage put the scales on the counter and told her to put what gold she had in one of the pans, then he balanced it with raisins. I asked him if raisins were worth their weight in gold and he said, 'Oh, well, she doesn't want the gold; she wants the raisins.' . . . Savage was always causing trouble among the Indians."[2] Savage was also less than generous with the white miners, who were forced to accept his high prices for goods in order to save the time it would have cost them if they'd traveled into the village of Mariposa.

Savage's rapport with the Indians deteriorated even more following a trip to San Francisco in October 1850 with two of his Indian wives. J. M. Cunningham, who also accompanied Savage, claimed, "One of the first causes of the Mariposa Indian War was a difficulty which arose between . . . Savage and an Indian . . . called Jose Juarez [who was] of some note in the Tribes about the Chowchilla and Fresno Rivers and had influence in those Tribes." After a long evening of heavy drinking, Savage and Juarez argued violently. Cunningham said that Savage struck Jose, whose intoxication was an embarrassment to him. He continued, "I frequently heard the Indian mutter threats of what he would do when he got back to his own people, but when sober he concealed his anger and Indian like waited his opportunity for revenge."[3]

Dr. Lafayette Houghton Bunnell's impression of these events differed. He claimed that Savage was drunk. "Jose arose, apparently sober, and from that time maintained a silent and dignified demeanor," Bunnell wrote in his personal memoirs.[4]

Jose Rey, who was also identified as a Chowchilla leader but who may have been a Chukchansi, sided with Juarez after he heard about the dispute. Both men stopped trading with Savage and began inciting the area's several tribes to drive the white people away. Although Nɨm families lived only a few miles over the ridge from Grub Gulch, there is no evidence they became involved in the disagreement.

Adam Johnston, who in April 1849 was appointed Indian agent for the Sacramento and San Joaquin River areas, journeyed to Savage's Fresno River trading post in the fall of 1850 to try to appease several tribal headmen, including Rey, Juarez, a man identified as Vouchester (who was sometimes called Baptista), and Tomkit, a leader of the Dumna who lived in the eastern San Joaquin Valley foothills near the San Joaquin River. He was apparently unsuccessful, as by mid-December unidentified Indians attacked and murdered three clerks at the Fresno River trading post, burning the post to the ground. Mariposa County officials did not act then against the Indians, because they assumed the attack was a continuation of Savage's personal dispute with Juarez. Unfortunately, their wisdom was soon tainted.

Savage did not know his attackers, yet he used the incident to gather together and incite nearby miners, warning them to arm themselves as quickly as possible against the Indians. Johnston also joined the fray, fueling the miners' fears by falsely warning them that an Indian attack was imminent. Although no miners had been killed, the miners were encouraged to kill all Indians, regardless of their guilt or innocence. Johnston knew that most of the Indians (who were probably from the Miwok tribe) had left their homes near the community of Mariposa to hide in the mountains; yet he petitioned California's Gov. Peter H. Burnett to protect the miners.

Soon after statehood the California legislature approved "An Act for the Government and Protection of the Indians," which permitted white farmers to indenture (read: enslave) Indians. The act would have enabled even the miners to indenture Indians. But that's not what they wanted. They wanted the Indians' land, and they were ready to fight for it.

Military campaigns had already been waged against northern California Indians who were impeding mining interests there. Thus, in January 1851, there was no legislative resistance when Governor Burnett ordered a war of extinction against the Indians, the unavoidable and "inevitable destiny" of the Indian people. When Burnett resigned before he could put words into action, Sheriff James Burney asked the new governor, John McDougal, for permission to "subjugate" the mountain tribes, from the Tuolumne River north of the village of Mariposa to the Tejon Pass in the Tehachapi Mountains, at the southern extremity of the San Joaquin Valley.

But Burney was impatient. Acting on his own authority, he solicited miners to form a volunteer militia to protect the frontier after the Indians at Coarsegold and Fine Gold, the head of the San Joaquin, and the Four Creeks region appeared to be hostile. Burney led a large party of armed miners in an attack against any Indians they encountered. His scout was James Savage.

Savage's recent military experience in northern California now served him well. He assumed leadership of another contingent that traveled toward Pilot Peak, south of the village of Mariposa. He also appointed a miner, "S. Skeane," to the rank of lieutenant in a hastily organized military organization called Company 1, California Volunteers. Skeane led an attack on a group of Indians near Pilot Peak who, according to Savage, were from marauding foothill tribes. "Without the least delay," Bunnell wrote, "the men dashed in and with brands from the camp fire, set the wigwams burning, and at the same time madly attacked the now alarmed camp. . . . Jose Rey [Savage's sworn enemy] was among the first shot down."[5] Rey evaded capture after Skeane was mortally wounded. The miners withdrew.

Skeane became the miners' hero, the first "soldier" killed in the conflict. In fact, he may have died from a shot fired by another miner. "Bad blood had developed between two of the men in the party," recalled Dorsey Ramsden in an interview, "and in the dusk and confusion one man's gun was fired. . . . As a result of the shot . . . Lieutenant Skeene [sic] was fatally wounded and another seriously injured."[6]

Savage next claimed that all the miners south of the village of Mariposa had been killed by Indians, and he instructed Burney to arrange a meeting in Mariposa. The seventy-five miners who attended drafted and signed a petition demanding that Burney brand all Indians outlaws and permit the miners to kill Indians throughout Mariposa County. The only condition was that bodies had to be buried and the sheriff informed of the location and number of Indians killed. At that time, Cha:tiniu was within Mariposa County's boundaries.

This deadly philosophy, "There's no good Indian but a dead Indian," fueled the mountain Indians' fear of white men for years afterward. Indian people would disappear without a trace; and each family had its own stories of rape and beating. Grandma said her parents hid their children whenever people came to their home. She'd hide Gloria and me when we were children. "Go, hide," she'd order us when white people came to the house. My great-grandfather, Jim Moore, was found dead in 1948, behind a North Fork business. The family suspected that he was beaten to death by white men, but in those days law enforcement officers weren't interested in Indians' opinions. Caution in their relationship with non-Indians prevails among some Nɨm families even today.

Meanwhile, back in Washington, D.C., the federal government saw another frontier to be conquered and settled as the nation expanded across the continent. At the request of California's mining and farming interests, the government implemented its own Indian policies based on local interests. It turned to the long-established treaty process initiated in 1789, when the management of the nation's Indian affairs was delegated to the War Department. In 1793 Congress invalidated all Indian title to lands not formerly acquired by treaty under the Constitution and placed Indian matters directly in the president's hands. Congress's intent was to extinguish Indian title to the public domain through treaties with individual tribes while at the same time effectively removing the Indians from the advancing frontier by placing them on federal reservations located in areas chosen by the government.

Thousands of California's acres were prime land ripe for settlement by American pioneers but lived on by numerous Indian tribes. In 1850 President Millard Fillmore appointed Redick McKee, Oliver W. Wozencraft, and George W. Barbour as his representatives and commissioned them to journey overland to California to meet and treaty with Indian tribes living in important gold mining regions in the San Joaquin Valley and the western Sierra Nevada. Indians living along the coast or in California's eastern deserts weren't involved. The government assumed the Indians wouldn't resist relinquishment of their right to ancestral lands in exchange for reservation land and sundry goods.

Erasmus D. Keyes was a West Point graduate and career army officer, most recently appointed by Gen. Persifer F. Smith to the rank of captain in command of the artillery company at the post of San Francisco. Keyes was detached to assist the commissioners in their negotiations with the tribes. He was also secretly armed by the War Department's General Hitchcock to, if necessary, subdue the Indians with force. A trained force of two hundred infantry soldiers from Companies M and F of the 3d Artillery Regiment and Companies B and K of the 2d Infantry were placed under his command. Keyes led the commissioners south from San Francisco through the San Joaquin Valley, through pristine country coveted by the federal government for its public domain.

Others, meanwhile, were marshaling for an Indian attack. Burney finally received the governor's edict to raise a military force. Two hundred miners volunteered and were hastily organized as the Mariposa Battalion. They were ordered to subdue, capture, and remove all the Indians living in Mariposa County to a reservation in the foothills on the Fresno River.

Savage was elected the battalion's leader; he immediately assumed the military title of major. Burney wasn't too pleased about that, as he also wanted to lead the battalion. But he'd already declined an appeal by the miners to lead them, publicly pleading his position as county sheriff and claiming to respect Savage's fluency in several Indian languages. He also had knowledge of the countryside, Burney said.

Years later, however, Burney recalled his loss of confidence in Savage in a March 20, 1885, letter to J. M. Hutchings, who was gathering information for a work on early California:

[Savage] . . . told me confidentially that he desired to go even with a small force . . . and if the Indians cut his men all to pieces it would incite the Americans so that they would turn out in sufficient force to conquer the Indians and then he could get control of them again and all he wanted was to work them one more season in the mines and he would have all the money he wanted. . . . I thought . . . he would not do to trust.[7]

The volunteer miners were now militiamen and were paid $4 a day for each private, up to $12 a day for Savage. They gathered about two miles south of the village of Mariposa to await orders. While there, they were further inflamed when they learned of attacks by unidentified Indians against teamsters near Fine Gold Gulch and the death of trader Wiley P. Cassady at his San Joaquin River store on the former Castro land grant.

A few Indian families, meanwhile, traveled to Camp Fremont, a temporary tent encampment established for the commissioners in the lower foothill drainage of the Mariposa River, on Fremont's La Purisima Ranch. A festive air prevailed on Sunday, March 9, as visitors from the surrounding area arrived to see the Indians, commissioners, and soldiers. More Indians arrived during the next few days, and a treaty was signed with six of their leaders on March 19.

The commissioners then sent word to all of the remaining mountain "warriors" including the "Monos," some of whom had refused to come in, to report to Camp McLean with their families by the end of March, to sign a treaty. This camp was another hastily established tent "fort" on the banks of the Fresno River, where the valley plains blend with the lowest foothills, between present-day Adobe Ranch and Hensley Lake. At the same time, however, the Mariposa Battalion was finally ordered into what became a month-long campaign to subdue those Indians who refused to come into the fort and transport them to Camp McLean, where the reservation would be established.

The "monos" most often referred to in the historical reports of the early 1850s were actually that portion of Chief Tenaya's band living at that time in Yosemite Valley. Tenaya's lineage was part sibiti Nɨm and part Ahwaneechee from Yosemite Valley. Accompanied by others, Tenaya left his family and established himself as a chief in Yosemite. He refused to surrender and escaped to his family on the eastern slope, where he and his followers were eventually captured.

The miners hoped for a quick and final conclusion to the "Indian problem," but that was not to be. Sorties again swarmed over the countryside, searching fruitlessly for the recalcitrant Chowchilla. Savage returned to Camp McLean on April 2 and joined forces with Keyes. An unidentified correspondent, after meeting with two Mariposa Battalion officers in San Jose on April 22, 1851, penned his observations.

> This [the Chowchilla], the most powerful of the Indian tribes in California, is believed to have at its command 1000 warriors. A portion of the Pyanches [the eastern Mono of today] from the other side of the Sierras are known to be allied with them and other tribes this side of the mountains [alluding to the presence of Tenaya]. A hard fight is anticipated with them since they have refused all overtures of peace and have committed the most daring robberies and unprovoked murders in the neighborhood of fine and coarse Gold Gulches. Large quantities of snow have fallen since the expedition started, which will render the march exceedingly difficult. . . . [T]he Major and the officers . . . will not turn back for any ordinary difficulties, and we may expect soon to hear of the complete subjection of the Chow-chillas. . . . The best of feeling exists between the regular and volunteer forces, and in the course of a month it is believed the Indian difficulties will be satisfactorily settled from the Calaveras to the Tulare Lake, *opening to miners some of the best mining and agricultural districts in the state.*[8]

To escape the advancing soldiers, some of the Chowchilla retreated southeast into the Sierras, toward the isolation of Cha:tiniu, where they expected to be welcomed by the Nɨm. The Nɨm's act of friendship was ultimately disastrous.

April 14, 1851, dawned. The Mariposa Battalion, some of whom rode horseback, marched with panache. Eccleston wrote,

> We made a display at once formidable & romantic. . . . [A] young squaw who is acting as guide . . . was mounted on a large Rowen horse & sat astradle & rode without stirrups. She wore a hat under which her black & straight hair hung down gracefully upon her shoulders, which were partially covered with a scarf thrown negligently over the left shoulder, her bodice was white muslin & her skirt of blue fig[ured] calico, & her small feet & ankles showed to advantage. Next to her, Major Savage rode . . . & . . . the whole Battalion in Indian file making a formidable appearance, each carrying their Red, blue &c. blankets behind them & our youthful Guidess would every little while look back & seem proud of her station.[9]

Indian scouts from an unidentified San Joaquin Valley tribe led the soldiers eastward into the mountains. Savage's plan was to sweep the area of scattered bands as he followed a circuitous route. For three days they followed Coarsegold Gulch to the headwaters of the Fresno River, crossing over today's Goat Mountain, and entered a lush valley rich with abundant game and acorns.

The battalion had arrived in Nɨm territory, where the animal people awaited them. "As we entered the valley selected for our camping place, a flock of sand-hill cranes rose from it with their usual persistent yells; and from this incident, their name was affixed to the valley and is the name by which it is now known," wrote Bunnell.[10] It is still known as Crane Valley. Grandpa said cranes are always the first into battle.

The scouts rendezvoused with the main force near a double waterfall at the west end of the lush valley, where the grass was good, there was an abundance of soap root for washing, and a placid stream ran through rich meadowland. The stream was named the

North Fork of the San Joaquin River, but some years later, after its own headwaters were discovered, it was renamed Willow Creek. Many deer, bear, and a variety of small animals were hunted for food. The soldiers searched for Indians in the valley and surrounding mountains but found nothing, except for a few tracks on the trail. Some of the soldiers expressed an interest in laying claim to Crane Valley for a ranch, after the Indians were conquered.

Members of Mom's paternal family were fortunate that the whole valley wasn't explored. Several Nïm families lived a few miles downstream, among them the ancestors of great-grandma Kitty Camino, who married great-grandpa Dick Pomona. Grandma Kitty's nephew, Dan McSwain, recalled living as a child, early in the twentieth century, in a cedar bark house at what is now known as Willow Cove. His homesite, Grandma Kitty's homesite, the battalion's campsite, and much of Crane Valley including a broad meadow around which Nïm families built their cedar bark homes have all disappeared beneath Willow Creek's impounded water. The area is known today as Bass Lake, a popular water sport, vacation, and retiree locale. Only occasionally, during a dry winter, does the original scene that greeted the Mariposa Battalion become vaguely visible, when Willow Creek flows so slowly that the lake's level lowers and the creek flows as it did long ago. The double waterfall still invites exploration. Cranes still nest in tall snags around the lake, flying overhead in search of food. Bears and mountain lions are occasionally sighted, and deer still roam Crane Valley. Absent from the scene are the Nïm, although Grandpa Dan, over ninety years old, lives just a few miles away from his boyhood home, his memories of his early years in Crane Valley still vivid.

Savage was recalled to the commissioners' headquarters; before leaving he ordered John Bowling, another miner who volunteered for the battalion and was immediately appointed "captain" of Company B, to take command and follow the elusive Indians. Sandino, a Mission Indian, whom Bowling later accused of inefficiency and cunning, stayed behind to guide and interpret.

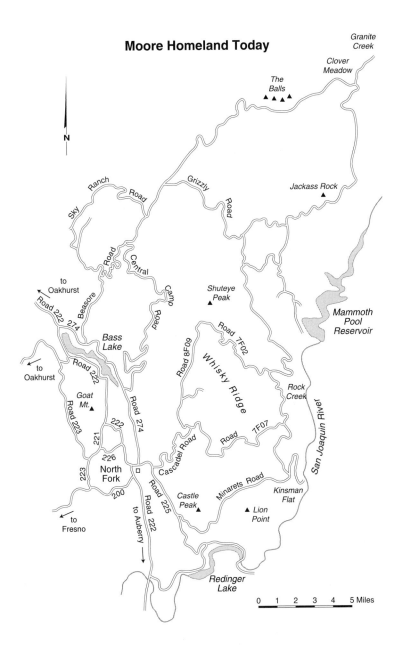

Moore Homeland Today

Granite
Creek

Clover
Meadow

The
Balls

Jackass Rock ▲

Sky Ranch Road

Grizzly Road

Beasore Road

Central Camp Road

to
Oakhurst

Road 222

274

Bass
Lake

to
Oakhurst

Road 222

Goat
Mt. ▲

Road 223

221

222

Road 274

226

223

North
Fork

200

to
Fresno

Road 225

to Auberry

Shuteye
Peak ▲

Road 7F02

Road 8F09

Whisky Ridge

Road 7F07

Cascadel Road

Castle
Peak ▲

Minarets Road

▲ Lion
Point

Mammoth
Pool
Reservoir

Rock
Creek

San Joaquin River

Kinsman
Flat

Redinger
Lake

0 1 2 3 4 5 Miles

N

An estimated one hundred soldiers started out, slogging in heavy rain, higher and higher into the mountains. They camped at night with their horses in pristine meadows that were quickly fouled and trampled. Following what became known as Beasore Creek, they traveled through meadows yet to be named Johnson and Arnold, out onto the sharp ridge between the not-yet-named Chiquito Creek and the west fork of the San Joaquin River. They reached the upper San Joaquin River on April 25, only to discover an abandoned settlement in the area of Cha:tiniu.

Hardy adventurers can follow some of the battalion's route. A pickup truck journey over rutted dirt roads took us one day to Little Shuteye Pass at the base of Shuteye Peak, past which the battalion traveled. The vista draws the eye northeast, into the Sierras. Less hardy travelers can enjoy a springtime exploration on a macadam highway that meanders through the forest, beginning at The Pines Village on the north shore of Bass Lake, past brilliantly flowered meadows, beneath a canopy of old growth trees, along briskly flowing creeks. It is easy, if not pleasant, to visualize the past: Nɨm living throughout the forest, their stores of hundreds of pounds of acorns and pine nuts, their homes, all torched by the soldiers.

"On arriving at the [San Joaquin] river it was found to be very deep," Bowling wrote. "A large Indian ranch and playground, with some few Indians standing about was discovered on the opposite side."[11] The soldiers were poised at Yoninau, a traditional Nɨm river crossing, where some Indians—who could have been either the escaping Chowchilla or Nɨm from the immediate area—had just evaded them, crossing the river by holding onto a woven rope that was later cut down by "some of the boys." The soldiers used their horses' ropes to lash together a few dry pieces of timber and fashioned a flimsy raft on which some soldiers crossed to the other side. Others swam. Bowling continued:

The water was as cold as ice, and rushed down the canyon with such rapidity as to apparently defy a passage. . . . There was no dallying, the Indians were in sight and the boys appeared not to know there was any obstacle in their way. No sooner was the word given than their clothing was off, and all the good swimmers rushed into the foaming current.

The Indians hollered at the swimming soldiers as they disappeared into the brush and rocks. Sandino was suspected of alerting them to the battalion's approach. The soldiers were now without horses.

> Preparations were immediately made for battle, which resulted in a foot race. The whole force, as near abreast as circumstances would admit, slowly and cautiously ascended the mountain, each step expecting to hear the hum of an arrow, until we arrived at the rancheria. No Indians were to be found. They had only left a few minutes, making large trails in different directions, and having nearly all their provisions and some clothing. This village consisted of about one hundred and fifty huts, and a large supply of acorns, all of which we destroyed, being satisfied that the men were secreted among the bushes watching our movements. I sought to ascertain in what direction the women and children had gone, that we might pursue them, and probably bring the men into a fight.

The soldiers found only the remains of a fire at the abandoned settlement. Sandino sifted the ashes, finding what he claimed was Jose Rey's knife. He also identified some bones as those of the mortally wounded Rey. Whether it was Rey or someone else from another tribe, the Nɨm would not have hesitated to perform the mourning ceremony, to be paid for their services with trade items.

For several more days the Nɨm continued to scatter in advance of the relentless soldiers, who continued to burn settlements and acorn stores. Disgust quickly replaced elation when the soldiers found only occasional tracks and sighted only a couple of Indians in the distance. Sandino suggested the soldiers' quarry had escaped by swimming back across the boiling river.

More days passed in a fruitless search as the Nɨm continued to withdraw, leading the soldiers toward the region that would be named Kaiser Pass. The soldiers occasionally observed women and children outdistancing them in a fast march eastward, deeper into the mountains. I can't help but wonder if Chinitit was one of them.

Finally, as the Nɨm continued to evade them and their supplies dwindled, the soldiers retreated. The trail became more difficult as they were forced to scramble over huge boulders and through heavy brush; one misstep or slip could have hurled a man several hundred feet into the river. When they finally reached the river crossing, the soldiers found their raft so soaked only one man at a time could cross. Suddenly some soldiers still on the opposite side began to shoot across the river where Nɨm were signing that they wanted to parley but instead fired their arrows. The soldiers shot four of them.

The bow and arrow was the usual weapon of warfare of my ancestors in the 1850s, although some Nɨm were known to have guns, probably old muskets taken from the Spaniards and Mexicans in earlier decades. Bunnell wrote,

> The self-confident and experienced . . . men . . . felt annoyed that these Indians had escaped when almost within range of our rifles. Our feelings—as a military organization—were irritated by the successful manner in which they had eluded our pursuit, and thrown us from their trail. We had been outwitted by these ignorant Indians; but as individuals, no one seemed inclined to acknowledge it.[12]

Tired and cold, the soldiers retreated westward out of the Sierras to the San Joaquin River, near where Cassady's store had been. Keyes and his regular soldiers had created a tent encampment there for the commissioners, on a narrow plain near a village of "friendly" Indians. It was a comforting sight for the weary battalion, the surrounding hills bright green and with patches of brilliantly colored spring wildflowers. The encampment was named Camp Barbour.

On April 29 messengers were sent to the remaining foothill Indians to announce a peace parley. If they surrendered, the Indians were promised food, clothing, and protection. If they refused, they were promised extermination.

There was a festive air as an estimated 1,200 people from a number of local tribes assembled. Many had never seen a white man. Keyes was impressed with their general appearance. He watched the Indians amuse themselves playing games and sports.

Three men whom the commissioners identified as principal chiefs of the tribes negotiated a handwritten treaty with the commissioners on April 29, 1851, on behalf of sixteen tribes representing an alleged four thousand Indians. The feared mountain Indians, who could have been Tenaya's band or the Nɨm of the upper San Joaquin River, were absent. The treaty provided for their anticipated arrival.

> And it is expressly understood that the *mona* or wild portion of the tribes . . . which are still out in the mountains, shall, when they come in, be incorporated with their respective bands . . . and the tribes above named pledge themselves to use their influence and best exertions to bring in and settle the said monas at the earliest possible day; and when the Yo-semi-te tribe comes in they shall in like manner be associated with the tribes or bands under the authority or control of Naiyak-qua.[13]

By agreeing to the treaty's provisions, Indian leaders hoped to protect their people against continued attacks by soldiers; instead, they effectively destroyed their tribes' traditional lifestyle. There is no evidence that any Nɨm leader signed the treaty or that any Nɨm who lived deep in the Sierras were forced from their homeland.

The "Tom quit" who signed the treaty was Tomkit, the aged chief of the Dumna (identified in the treaty as Toomnas) who, after he assumed leadership of the dissidents when Jose Rey was wounded, vowed to fight Savage rather than surrender. The recollections of an aged man, Pahmit, who was Tomkit's twenty-nine-year-old grandson when the treaty was signed, paint a scenario at odds with the historical picture.

The Dumna were a content people before the soldiers arrived, Pahmit recalled. They had plenty to eat and comfortable homes at Kuyu Illik, their encampment near the treaty grounds. San Joaquin River miners were the first white men Pahmit saw.

Pahmit watched as Savage, dressed in blue clothes and riding a horse, entered Camp Barbour accompanied by several other armed and mounted men. "I big medicine man with big father at Washington," Pahmit recalled Savage's words. "You haf do what I say. I hurt you if I want to [Savage's allusion to the magical powers afforded him by his gun]."[14] Deciding it was in his people's best interest to obey Savage, Tomkit gathered the other chiefs together to meet with the commissioners at Camp Barbour.

Yo-ho, a California mission-educated Indian who once lived with the Dumna, was the commissioners' translator during the treaty negotiations. At first the Indians didn't like what they heard and refused to negotiate, Pahmit recalled. So the commissioners decided to appease the leaders by smoking tobacco with them. "Then Major Savage give 'em lots whiskey. . . . Then they make sign mark on piece paper. . . . Lots Indian sign 'em."[15]

More trouble was brewing. "There are parts of 2 or 3 tribes which would not come in to treat," wrote an unidentified correspondent for the *Daily Alta Californian*.[16] The commissioners ordered Savage and three companies to move against them. They still thought they were dealing with Tenaya's band, but they were again back in Nim territory. Even Eccleston was concerned: "There was considerable threats about disturbing the peaceable Indians by the discomfitted party."[17] But it was too late. Savage left Camp Barbour in early May, determined to capture the recalcitrant Indians.

There were actually two engagements. Bowling's command went

to the Yosemite Valley to capture Tenaya. He was guided by Cow-Chitty, an Indian scout in whom Savage placed great faith, as he was an old enemy of Tenaya. Savage commanded the remaining soldiers, following the battalion's earlier route to Crane Valley and onward into the mountains. They camped on May 7 at a very large abandoned settlement on a ridge known today as Forked Meadow, between the west fork of the San Joaquin River and the Chiquito, or little San Joaquin, near Cha:tiniu.

The soldiers advanced, camping along the trail at other recently abandoned settlements, at places now named Jackass Meadow and Soldier Meadow. Grandpa John said he knew this "old trail" when I explained the war to him. He said he'd walked it with his dad, Jim Moore, years ago.

Near the upper north fork of the San Joaquin River the soldiers found tracks of Indians who were retreating as they advanced, but they had difficulty following them. Campfires were seen in the distance, but the soldiers couldn't reach them. Then they faced what appeared to be impassable boulders but found long poles that the Indians had placed from one large boulder to another. Grapevines were attached above the poles and stretched a short distance apart, then fastened together by smaller vines, enabling the Indians to walk the poles while holding onto the grapevines. The soldiers followed.

The soldiers advanced deeper and deeper into the mountains. As during the earlier attempt, Indians were seen across the river, but Savage realized his command was unprepared to pursue them. They retreated, along the way again burning hundreds of bushels of acorns and pine nuts, and arrived at Camp Barbour on May 17. Once again, my ancestors evaded the enemy.

A few days later news reached Camp Barbour that Bowling had successfully captured Tenaya and his band, including three of Tenaya's sons, in the Yosemite Valley. One son was killed trying to escape. (Tenaya spent a year in captivity. After he was released, he traveled across the Sierras to join relatives near Mono Lake, where he was killed during a dispute with some of his own tribe.)

Within the next few weeks leaders of other foothill tribes south of the San Joaquin River also signed treaties. Their relinquishment of their foothill homeland, coupled with the treaty that embraced Nɨm territory, placed thousands more acres in the public domain. A correspondent wrote in a July 30, 1865, letter, "And I am happy to add . . . that the country is fast filling up with an industrious American population. . . . If any of your readers should desire to emigrate to, and settle in, that beautiful section of the State, enjoying as it does a most delicious and healthy climate, they will find an abundance of good land yet to be possessed."[18]

After the commissioners left Camp Barbour, Keyes led the 2d Infantry a short distance to a new camp on the San Joaquin River, where they were joined within a few days by Lieutenants Moore and McLean. The soldiers built a log outpost that was named Fort Miller to enforce the treaty and protect the mining districts by controlling the Indians between the Merced and Kern rivers.

Pahmit's recollections again differ with the historical record. He claimed that some of the Dumna remained at their ancestral home after the treaty was signed.

> After 'wile soldiers come, make big wood house for fight. They all got gun. They catch lots Indian. Some Indian get 'way. . . . My grandpa, Tomkit, tell soldiers, "Put away gun; my people come in; they no like gun." Sometimes the soldiers whipped the Indians into building the wood house. . . . They whip, whip, whip. Two, three Indian die—whip'em too much. . . . They run all Indian 'way from village Kuyu Illik. They burn all Indian house.[19]

Pahmit said his dad also warned, "Indian spirits no like you do this. Pretty soon bad things happen to you."[20] The San Joaquin River overran its banks soon afterwards, Pahmit added, washing away a store, killing some Chinese men, and forcing some of the soldiers to leave. In the Sierra Nevada foothills, along the San Joaquin, Fresno, and Chowchilla rivers, many miners became sick. The federal government hired forty doctors to travel to the affected areas to treat those suffering with fever and other maladies, but some of the men died.

Finally, early that summer, after the federal government was convinced that the Indians were controlled, the volunteer Mariposa Battalion was mustered out of service. Some federal troops remained at Fort Miller because Barbour was concerned that continuing misdeeds by miners could once again inflame the Indians.

At Cha:tiniu, Chinitit and her family reclaimed their life. They built new tonobi and granaries. They had to wait until fall, though, to gather bushels upon bushels of acorns and to wait until winter to gather material to replace the many baskets burned in the fires. At least there was some food. Their dried meat had been destroyed, but there were the seeds and bulbs of spring, stream fish, fresh deer meat, and a variety of small animals. It may have been during this period that an itinerant miner taught my family to pan gold from the San Joaquin River and nearby creeks.

After the war ended, some miners continued to explore the San Joaquin River. They moved deeper into the Sierra Nevada until they reached a creek east of the river, near Cha:tiniu, where they discovered gold. To recover the gold they had to use large hydraulic nozzles to wash away the hillside soil in a ravine they called Kaiser Gulch. A small settlement soon rose nearby, clinging to the side of the ravine. By 1852 or 1853 the mining district was known as the Kaiser Diggings, but the absence of a wagon road prevented its growth, and the Kaiser district took its place in history. Also nearby, in the 1850s, partners named Harris and Wolff and a man named Logan opened stores so they could trade their "Digger ounce" for commodities.

Grandpa John enjoyed reminiscing about his youth in the mid-teens of the twentieth century, when he and his dad rode horseback from their home at Peyakinu over the ridge to the San Joaquin River to pan for gold. Mom, too, remembers when she was a young girl going with her grandparents, Jim and Lizzie Moore, for a day's outing to pan gold from the river and its tributaries. Usually, she said, they found enough gold dust to buy groceries when they made their periodic horse-drawn wagon trips into North Fork.

Elsewhere in our territory, however, some of the Nɨm who lived near Crane Valley, at Fine Gold Creek, or in the foothills bordering the San Joaquin River may have been forced onto a reservation in the foothills. Although my ancestors avoided imprisonment there, the mentality that created the reservation eventually resulted in Chinitit's descendants adapting their lifestyle to the white man's.

The treatied Indians' new home was intended to be a 50-mile-long-by-15-mile-wide strip of generally poor foothill land between the Chowchilla and Kaweah rivers in the eastern San Joaquin Valley. The actual reservation was much smaller. It was officially named the Fresno River Farm, but as the years passed it was more often called the Fresno River Reservation or Reserve. Its eastern boundary was the site of an Indian rancheria located below the confluence of the Fresno River and Coarsegold Creek which was overtaken by the battalion and where the commissioners had bivouacked at Camp McLean. To the west the reservation included all the land to just beyond Highway 145. Through the reservation flowed the Fresno River.

By signing the treaty tribal leaders agreed that their followers would live peacefully and in friendship with their conqueror, and if accosted by white men, the leaders promised not to retaliate, leaving to the government the settling of their affairs. The federal government also promised to give the treatied Indians beef cattle, farm animals, agricultural tools, and clothing. A farmer, a blacksmith, a carpenter, and a schoolteacher were to live with the Indians, teaching land cultivation in exchange for the wheat and flour the Indians produced.

By early summer hundreds of people from most of the treatied tribes were living and farming on the reservation. It was the worst of land. Its rolling hills were unsuitable for the farming techniques the Indians were to be taught, and it was much hotter than their former homes in the higher elevations. Only where today's Adobe Ranch borders the Fresno River west of Hensley Lake does the land settle into plains conducive to farming; but it lacked the kinds of vegetation that had nurtured the Indians for centuries.

The reservation's management was a sham. Indians worked as slaves for their overseers rather than as farmers. Savage and his partners—several miners who had served in the Mariposa Battalion—operated a store on the north bank of the Fresno River, near the Indians' homes. Another partner was the reservation's superintendent, headquartered at Fort Bishop, just west of today's Adobe Ranch.

Savage made a deal with his friend Fremont, who was back in California after serving several years in the U.S. Senate following his 1849 election from California. Fremont sold beef to Savage, who resold the animals to the federal government for the Indians. One of Savage's employees, Joel H. Brooks, eventually accused him of doctoring the receipts so as to earn a considerable profit from the enterprise:

> My instructions from Savage were that when I delivered cattle on the San Joaquin and King's river, . . . I was to take receipts for double the number actually delivered, . . . and when to Indians on the Fresno, to deliver one-third less than were receipted for. . . . I also had orders to sell all beef I could to miners . . . and to deliver cattle to his clerks, to be sold to Indians on the San Joaquin, at twenty-five cents per pound; and I know that such sales were made to these Indians.[21]

There were other deals: Savage paid $1,000 to federal authorities for a trading license and constructed several buildings on the reservation. He also hired former battalion soldiers to help run the business.

The Indians were allowed to dig gold from the Fresno River, but they were forced to give up their meager gleanings in exchange for the clothing they were promised but never received. Savage also reaped profits from settlers who bartered at his trading post after they established farms and ranches immediately outside the farm's boundaries. And Savage lived near the post with some of his Indian "wives."

Also that summer miners entered the reservation to search the Fresno River for gold. Fearing that the treaty would fail if the reservation Indians reacted, federal authorities sent Lt. Tredwell Moore to close businesses operated by unauthorized traders at the reservation and at Fort Miller, and he ordered the angry miners to leave. They didn't. George Barbour, who was now an Indian agent, made several trips from Fort Miller to the reservation before he was able to calm the Indians. He was only able to convince a few miners to leave.

There was more deception. Charles E. Mix, a federal commissioner of Indian affairs, informed Barbour that any untreatied tribes who signed additional treaties in 1851 would receive only the right to live at the reservation. They would not be given clothing or food.

The final blow was struck when California's legislature successfully lobbied the U.S. Senate to reject the eighteen treaties, claiming that by establishing reservations embracing thousands of acres from the public domain the federal government was effectively depriving the non-Indians of valuable agricultural and mineral land. Not only were the treaties never ratified, the Senate's action was cloaked in silence after any documents pertaining to it were sealed. But, at the request of California's Sen. John B. Weller, the U.S. Senate did appropriate $100,000 for the Indians' "temporary relief," enabling reservation officials to continue its management, which by this time was mostly for their own profit. Not until 1904, when the documents were unsealed, did California's Indians learn that they were betrayed and that, in fact, there were no reservations. It was too late. Their ancestral lands had been claimed as public domain for more than half a century.

Savage died suddenly and violently. Controversy dogged him

even in death. In the summer of 1852 Savage learned that Walter H. Harvey, another miner who was also a major in the Mariposa Battalion, may have been involved in attacks against Indians at the Kings River Reservation. Acting on the request of federal authorities at Fort Miller, Savage met with area Indians during a trip to the Four Creeks area. On August 16 he confronted Harvey, either at Harvey's ranch or on the Kings River Reservation. There are several versions of the incident, but all agree that harsh words were exchanged, fists flew, knives and guns were drawn, and Harvey shot Savage through the heart. Harvey was later acquitted of any wrongdoing.

Savage was buried at his trading post on the Fresno River Reservation. Some settlers, who considered Savage a hero, later erected a monument to him near the trading post to memorialize his role in settling the foothill country. They exhumed his bones from their original burial place and reburied them beneath the monument. In the 1970s, when it became apparent that the burial site would be flooded after the newly constructed Hidden Dam impounded the Fresno River, the U.S. Army Corps of Engineers disinterred the remains and reburied them yet again beneath the monument that was relocated to the Buck Ridge Recreation Area at Hensley Lake.

After Savage's death William Howard asserted that the widely publicized Indian attacks that caused the Mariposa Indian War were only "skirmishes" and that no one could prove that the Indians living in Mariposa had ever attacked white men. The Indians were misrepresented, he claimed, and made to appear hostile through Savage's actions.

Dr. George Stealey of San Francisco was the next trader licensed to operate the Fresno River Reservation's trading post. Violence continued when a band of white men murdered some of the reservation Indians. Not only were the white men never punished, their leader was later elected a county judge.

Foothill Indians, who evaded capture and internment at the reservation, continued to live in the mining areas. And they continued to face "occasional acts of violence on the part of a certain class of desperadoes [sic] who infest the mining regions of California, who regard oppression towards the weak as a merit, and with whom the life of an Indian, is valued only as that of a wild beast," reported Fort Miller's commanding officer, H. W. Wessells, in his March 7, 1852, report.[22]

Pasqual, a "Cho-e-nem-ne" leader who signed the Camp Barbour treaty, lamented in a translated statement printed in the *San Joaquin Republican* on July 21, 1852,

> What shall we do. We try to live on the land the Commissioners gave us in friendly relations with the whites, but they kill our women and children, and if we flee to the mountains, then they hunt us and kill us, and we have no peace on the lands the Commissioners give us, or in the mountains. Where shall we go and what shall we do? When the Commissioners gave us the United States flag and our papers, they told us that it would protect us, but now the Flag is all stained with our blood, and our papers are all bloody, the whites are rich and strong, and we pray for mercy. Our home has been taken from us, and we live on the lands the Great Father gave us, but how can we live here, and be innocently killed? . . . Intercede and protect us that we may live.[23]

Miners and settlers began to force some of the Indians off the Fresno River Reservation so as to gain control of the acreage. On March 3, 1853, President Millard Fillmore established five military reservations throughout California to which the state's Indians were to be moved "for subsistence and protection" of both Indians and white settlers. Edward Fitzgerald Beale was appointed an Indian commissioner to, among other duties, enforce the law. A military reserve, known as Sebastian Indian Reservation, was established later that year in the Tehachapi Mountains, at the Tejon Pass, south of the San Joaquin Valley. Almost one thousand Indians who lived east of the Sierra Nevada, in and near the Owens

Valley, were forcibly marched to that reservation, where they were given food, taught farming, and were to be protected by federal troops from marauding miners and settlers.

In the spring of 1854 Thomas J. Hensley, another former miner and soldier of the Mariposa Battalion and an early settler near the Fresno River Reservation, was appointed its administrator. He inherited many problems. Hensley saw the sorry conditions in which the Indians lived—destitute, suffering from disease and vice, their numbers greatly reduced since their arrival two years earlier. The only tribes still at the reservation were remnants of the Chowchilla, Chukchansi, Pohonochee, and Potohowchi tribes, who were now too ill to move to the Sebastian Indian Reservation. The rest had died or disappeared.

Meanwhile, still living high in the Sierra Nevada were Indians who continued to distrust white people and who continued to steal horses from the San Joaquin Valley. Some of these people, who were branded "hostiles," could have been my ancestors.

The Indians who were still living near Fort Miller suffered horrible conditions. Venereal disease swept through the troops stationed at the fort in the spring of 1857; many nearby Indians were also infected. When Captain Keyes returned to the fort in 1858 he learned that most of the Indians who had remained there had either died or become victims of alcohol.

It was inevitable. The Fresno River Reservation was officially abandoned on November 9, 1859, although some Indians remained there until 1861, when they were forcibly marched to other military reservations. A Dr. Leach then moved the trading post near Fort Miller.

No evidence of the 766,800-acre Fresno River Reservation remains. Much of the land is buried beneath Hensley Lake, a popular water recreation area developed by the U. S. Army Corps of Engineers when it built Hidden Dam in 1978 for flood control and irrigation. Also gone are the few remaining stones of the trading post that were still visible in the late 1960s.

In the early 1860s miners seeking gold at the San Joaquin River diggings and in creeks near Cha:tiniu relied on Jesse B. Ross to pack their supplies. Ross built a cabin for himself and his Indian woman, Wospi, whom he called Mary Wospi, at Nuyuha, later known as the Hogue Ranch. They had one child, Julia Belle, who remained with her father after Wospi left him.

Wospi went to live near relatives at, Saksakaniu, where she married Toku, my great-grandfather Dick Pomona's half-brother. Wospi's father, Penuwats, was a Wowa and a bohenab. Penuwats married a Nɨm woman, who was Wospi's mother; and even though he moved to Nɨm territory, he retained his hereditary position. Mom remembers Wospi, who, she said, was often called "Captain" by family and friends, a nickname likely given to her because of her father's position as a bohenab.

Ross remained at his ranch at Nuyuha, where he raised Julia Belle to adulthood. An apple orchard he planted there still produces fruit. In the 1890s Ross also farmed beans, providing employment to many Nɨm women who threshed the beans with a flail or round willow pole and winnowed them in baskets to separate the chaff. "My Grandma picked apples for him," Grandpa John recalled in his ninetieth year. "He [Ross] was an old man, bent over," was Grandpa John's childhood memory. "I wonder how many other of these people are married to Indian women, are using their Indian relations for labor as Ross did until he messed things up," wondered Joseph M. Kinsman.[24]

Kinsman arrived in California during the 1849 gold rush, hoping to make his fortune at several mining districts, the last attempt in the region around Millerton. In the 1870s he finally settled at Soyakinu, an area now known as Kinsman Flat, where he married one of my family's relatives, Maria Joaquin. Her family and friends called her Mary. Her descendants say she was well treated by her white husband.

Another war erupted in the 1860s, but this dispute was far from the events of the central Sierra Nevada. America's Civil War was under way. The federal government, determined that California would not join the Confederacy, reactivated Fort Miller, and a contingent of armed troops was posted there for a time to protect the Union's interests in the central San Joaquin Valley. Pahmit remembered this period, too.

> Then by 'n by, white man all talk fight. They say long way off, white man shoot white man. Lots white man go long way off, fight. Then white soldier come back Fort Miller. This time white soldier pretty good man; they no shoot Indian, they no whip Indian too much. Some Indian work for white soldier; white soldier give 'em flour, give 'em tobacco, but Indian pretty near all gone. . . . I big Chief now, but no got Indian tribe. . . . We work hard, we don't have 'nough eat. Big Father at Washington no send flour, no send horse; no send clothes; no send blanket like white chief say when Indian sign paper at Kuyu Illik.[25]

Toward the end of the Civil War William Brewer explored the Sierra Nevada. After leaving the Owens Valley, east of the Sierra Nevada, on August 2, 1864, he traveled westward through Mono Pass. Brewer's expedition followed an old Indian trail. "Smokes rise, when we start they appear, and at night their blaze is seen on the heights—so the Indians know all of our movements," he said.[26] They camped one night near the head of the middle fork of the San Joaquin River, where they met, without incident, eleven Indians armed with rifles traveling east.

The expedition continued a westerly trek, through country known to my family for centuries. On August 4, they camped in a broad, beautiful valley (later named Vermillion Valley) where, Grandma said, our ancestors traveled to each summer to bathe in the hot springs. "It is the stronghold of Indians; they are seldom molested here, and here they come when hunted out of the valleys," Brewer wrote.[27] They continued to see fires on the cliffs but no people. Still exploring westward along the San Joaquin River's middle fork, on August 15 their camp was close to Cha:tiniu. Six days later they camped at the head of "Chiquito Joaquin," also near Cha:tiniu.

Brewer wrote that, after continuing to descend from the higher elevations in a northwesterly direction, the expedition "finally struck some cattle trails, and, at length, the first dawn of civilization." He continued, "We found two men camped under a tree, watching cattle which they had driven up from the plains. . . . [The next day we] passed several cabins, in some of which white men were living with squaws, and a lot of half-breed 'pledges of affection' were seen."[28]

They camped that night by the Fresno River, near a white settler and his Indian woman, who gave them food. The area's oral history suggests they were at the Lewis Ranch, near today's Sky Ranch Road, east of Oakhurst. Here the explorers reversed their direction. They traveled east and on August 23, 1864, reached Clark's Ranch at Wawona. They had left Nɨm territory.

CHAPTER SIX

ENJOYING LIFE DURING PUHIDUWA

My ancestors continued to live at Cha:tiniu for at least a couple of decades after the Mariposa Battalion's attack. High in the sky Kwi'na watched and listened. The bohenab continued to guide the people, and from generation to generation the children of my family were taught the old ways, even until today.

During puhiduwa there is a time known as *isaduwa,* when coyote puppies are heard yapping, when, Grandpa said, the "others"—all those who are pregnant—are left alone. He'd say, "I tuwum bo pitchidɨ," "The children are sucking milk." These children of our "little brothers" wouldn't survive if we hunted during isaduwa. So for a while my family silences its weapons as the fledgling birds and the young of the animal world are nurtured and grow. It's OK to fish because the fish have already laid their eggs.

Does who are breeding and does with fawns are left alone, but the obviously barren doe is hunted. In the old days men would sweat before they hunted so the deer couldn't detect their human odor. The night before their planned hunt they entered the sweathouse, literally a bathhouse for cleansing the body; it is a semi-subterranean structure, dug about four feet underground, with a cedar bark roof constructed about three feet aboveground. After everyone went into the sweathouse soapstone rocks that had been heated in an outside fire pit until they were white-hot were carried inside with long sticks. Our family used only soapstone in the sweathouse, and also for cooking, as it is the rock least likely to explode after it becomes white-hot. Water was poured over the rocks to create steam, causing those inside to sweat profusely. After a half hour or so everyone came out and immediately jumped into the cold water of an adjacent stream or lake for the final cleansing. In later years, when the people were forced to live away from natural water sources, they poured pails of cold water over themselves to wash off the sweat.

Hunters shouldn't have sex the night before the hunt because it leaves an odor that deer can smell, Grandpa said. In the old days men rubbed their bodies with crushed wormwood leaves to confuse the deer; when the wind blew they smelled like the plant. Some of our family's hunters still observe these traditions.

Grandpa said that in the old days, to get close to the deer, hunters painted their lower legs white and wore antlers on their heads and deerskins over their shoulders. They held their bow and arrows in front of them with one end toward the ground so the weapons looked like the deer's forefeet. Then they shot, seldom missing their quarry.

Doe meat is the best tasting, sweeter and without as much muscle as the meat of bucks. Bucks were hunted year-round, except when they rutted in fall; then their meat was very tough. Some hunters ate the warm raw liver right after the kill because it builds strength. A young boy was expected to eat either the raw liver or raw fat from his first deer kill. I don't like the taste of raw fat, so I just eat the liver. Sometimes a young fawn was killed for an older person who didn't have many teeth but who could chew its very tender meat, Grandpa said. There were so many deer in the old days, he said, that the herds weren't endangered if a few fawns were killed.

Some fresh deer meat was roasted, but most of the meat was

dried on racks for later use. Freezers are used to preserve fresh meat today. The blood meat, where the arrow or bullet entered the body, was cut out and washed, mixed with other deer scraps, put into the stomach, and baked in a deep pit for delicious eating. Grandma cooked this way.

Now we just eat the meat, but in the old days every part of the deer was used. Antlers were fashioned into tools, muscle became sinew, brains were used for tanning, and skins were made into clothing and also used as doorway coverings. Grandpa showed me how easy it is to remove the hair from a deer skin before it is tanned. After soaking the skin for three days in water, he hand-rubbed a mixture of wood ashes and water onto the skin. Then the hair was easily rubbed off.

When the young fawns, squirrels, and rabbits no longer rely solely on their mothers for sustenance and begin to browse for food, it's time to resume hunting. No one needs to say, "OK, it's time to hunt." We were taught to watch and listen; all of our senses are equally important.

After I learned to walk Grandpa took me along when he hunted. And when I was eight years old he put a gun in my hand and taught me how to hunt. He said I was a man now. We'd roam the surrounding woods, Grandpa teaching me how and when to shoot. He showed me how to make and set traps, to track birds and animals. I learned what insects to eat. I also learned to speak and understand the animals' languages, to remain silent and still for minutes on end, watching. And, most important of all, Grandpa taught me to respect all living things, to thank them for caring for us, for providing us with food. I even learned why doves have pink feet.

Dove was married to Sun, Yohananahowi. She also was related to Coyote. Coyote was her brother-in-law. Dove and Sun were always fighting. Sun had a son, Chiwiwina. Sun was sleeping with another woman, Meadowlark. He fell in love with this woman, but Meadowlark didn't want him, but she kept pulling him to her by her hair.

Sun was in love with her anyway. Dove came and found them together. Yohananahowi knew he would be thrown out of the tribe for
this. He left Dove and took his son to a spring. Here he told his son
that no one wanted them, so they would go on to another world.
They sat at the spring singing a song, "Yohanana howi, yohanana
howi, yohanana howi, ebahu nɨkwa miyawai. Chiwiwina, chiwiwina, chiwiwina," and they stuck an arrow into the eye of the spring.
The spring opened up into a hole and Yohananahowi and Chiwiwina went into the eye, singing as they went. They walked for two
days. Yohananahowi and Chiwiwina heard some strangely familiar
noises. They heard the pounding of acorns and grinding of berries
and they smelled the cooking of meat. These people, the Wowa,
were getting ready for a big celebration, and they were going to have
a "big time," dancing, singing, and eating for four days. The Wowa
heard Chiwiwina and Yohananahowi coming and left their things as
they thought something bad was coming. The men banded together
and went after whatever was coming. They caught Chiwiwina and
Yohananahowi and brought them back to their village. They decided to go on with their celebration, but they would kill the two
strangers at the same time. The "big time" started and the dancing
and singing began. They tied Yohananahowi and Chiwiwina to a
stake. Yohananahowi and Chiwiwina watched all of the happenings
for three days. They knew that they would be killed tomorrow. They
were killed that morning and their heads were cut off. After they
were killed the people heard a big roar like that of ocean waves coming. This was Sun's uncle, Wind. Wind was singing a song while
coming: "Hi wai ya a. Hi wai ya a. Hi wai ya a. Hi wai ya a." Wind
was angry at the Wowa for killing his nephew, Sun. He was so strong
that when he arrived he threw the Wowa into the air and slammed
them to the ground. Everything was scattered all over and the only
thing that was left standing were Yohananahowi and Chiwiwina
who were still tied to the stake. Wind untied them and their bodies
fell to the ground. Wind split the bodies of Chiwiwina and Yohananahowi in two and both their halves came to life and all four of

them came out of the center of the earth. Coyote and Dove were sitting around a fire. Dove ran to Yohananahowi and hugged him. They were back together. Coyote was angry as he wanted Chiwiwina for a sister-in-law. He started to sing his sad song, crying at the same time, "Yowi hi ni, yowi hi ni, yowi hi ni, yowi hi ni." He turned to the north and said "Ehe-he." He grabbed Dove's two boys and threw them into the fire. He sang a song while dancing around, "Yo wi hi ni, yo wi hi ni, yo wi hi ni, yo wi hi ni." He thought he was going to kill them, but he didn't. The two little doves stumbled out of the fire. Their little feet were red. After their feet cooled, they turned pink. This is why doves have pink feet.   —as told by Grandma

Grandma taught us other lessons from this story: don't commit adultery or you will be killed; learn from the power of the elements, such as the wind.

When I was growing up Grandpa and I often went hunting for food; for rabbits, gray squirrels, marmots, and woodrats. The sky was filled with food: robins, mountain and valley quail, ducks, geese, and the mountain grouse. Grandpa said our family never hunts bear; she is our relative, an aunt. Once, he said, bighorn sheep were hunted "at the top of the mountain," alluding to the highest peaks of the Sierra Nevada, where these now-extinct animals were once lords of the crags. (The bighorn sheep still occasionally seen in the Sierra Nevada are not descendants of the original herd but were reintroduced in the 1980s by the California Department of Fish and Game.)

When I'm hunting I sometimes recall fragments of Grandpa's favorite hunting story, such as this one:

Coyote said laying down, "Mouse [his nephew], you call me when snow gets three feet. Then I go hunt Rabbit." "All right." It snow too high. Mouse said, "Now it's time." Coyote jumped up and had hell of time getting out. Mouse carried light on top of the snow to the mountain. "Come back. I want go down with you." Mice got inside

Mountain Sheep, killing him. Coyote said, "Throw me meat. I can't climb." So he threw his uncle the bones.

We used .22-caliber rifles for hunting, but Grandpa also taught me how to hunt with a bow and arrow. He preferred making his bows with wood from the bay tree; and we'd go to Kaiwaniga, a spring above Redinger Lake (just below it was a crossing of the San Joaquin River) to gather strong and straight branches from the buttonbush; they were perfect for forming arrows. The bowstring was made with two lengths of sinew from a deer's back-strap muscle. Grandpa would grip one end in his teeth and braid the two lengths together.

Grandpa's quiver held only a few arrows, but he had many arrowheads. He'd attach an arrowhead to a very short shaft he fashioned with strong young sticks from the black oak. The shafts were attached to the arrow; when the arrow was shot it separated from the shaft on impact. It was retrieved so it could be used over and over. Our arrowheads were made with obsidian traded from the Indians on the eastern slope of the Sierra Nevada.

Grandpa and I sat companionably together, our hands wrapped with deerskin and a skin over our thighs as we knapped obsidian into shape with a piece of deer antler. He showed me how to attach the finished arrowhead to the shaft with charcoal and pitch from the bull pine tree and then tie it securely with sinew. Grandpa said to use only sparrow hawk feathers to balance the arrow, attaching three of them spaced an equal distance apart. The sparrow hawk is so swift that it always catches its prey, Grandpa said; his arrows flew as swiftly as the bird, even around corners, he'd add. I always laughed when he said that. Whether hunting with a rifle or a bow and arrow, Grandpa taught me to always aim for the head, to shoot into the brain so the animal died instantly and didn't suffer.

Grandpa and I often drove down Road 225 toward Peyakinu, to hunt the scores of rabbits that scattered in all directions in front of us. I've hunted there over the years with great success. Early one evening, at the end of a hot summer day in 1994, I drove my wife in that direction, thinking it was time we shared a rabbit feast. We didn't see any rabbits near Peyakinu. A lot of people live near there now, and there's a lot of traffic to and from Redinger Lake.

"Them old people, they ate healthy," Mom reminisced nostalgically about her childhood. "No frying. Fresh roasted or boiled. We walked everywhere. Take dry jerky, put in your pocket and go for a walk. And we drank water from any place." Now many springs and streams are polluted.

Grandpa showed me how to shoot birds on the fly and how to catch them at night when they were sleeping. It was fun. I already knew where they nested, so after lighting a torch I'd sneak up on them, very quietly; when the birds were blinded by the light I'd grab them in my hand. Grandpa was such a stealthy hunter he could sneak up on an unsuspecting woodrat, even when it was awake, and grab it in his hand.

Have you ever observed the mountain and valley quail scurrying about, brushing the ground with their swiftly moving feet to uncover seeds, eating, then scurrying back into the brush for protection? I still make small brush piles near our home so I can watch their movements. In the old days hunters constructed long fences of chaparral brush to trap the unwary mountain and valley quail who sought protection in them. Grandpa showed me how to bend down a tender young shoot, preferably from the willow, and attach a trigger fashioned from a piece of hardwood and milkweed string. The bent twig was stuck in the ground inside small openings at several intervals in the brush fence. The unwary quail were caught by the snare and sprung into the air. Rabbits, gray squirrels, or other birds were also snared this way as they scurried along the ground. Grandpa and I checked our snares every two or three hours and were usually successful.

Newborn babies were given a quail's leg to suck on so they would be swift when they grew up. My daughter, Jacquie, did this, and a few years ago my grandson, Anthony, and my great-nephew,

Theodore, also sucked quail leg to give them speed when they are older.

Grandpa would watch the elms growing along the creeks. When their catkins started to get long and spread out, he knew it was time to go fishing. He taught me to fish about the same time he taught me to hunt. We fished for food, not for sport. We were fishing buddies, traveling to mountain streams to catch the "big ones" that never escaped Grandpa's touch.

Grandpa preferred fishing in lakes for rainbow trout and other trout varieties. I think that's boring, but it sure was exciting to watch him reel them in. He never used lures for bait, only live worms he dug at the spring near our house. He'd sit quietly, throwing his baited line overhead into the water, in the same way he would lasso an animal. One after another, Grandpa reeled in the fish. All around the lake other people were fishing, and waiting. Pretty soon, word was passed around about an old man's success, and people moved closer to fish near him. He continued to reel the fish in one after another. The other fishermen still waited. Grandpa's success wasn't due to any special expertise. He knew the fish were his equals, his sparring partners. He'd talk to them and listen to them. And he'd catch them. After he caught enough to eat he'd continue fishing, but he always threw the excess fish back instead of wasting them.

These days I enjoy the pure pleasure of stream fishing, leaping from boulder to boulder over the swiftly flowing water, finding deep holes near the rocks where the fish like to hide or hiding behind a boulder or tree, gently casting in my line, underhand, making my catch, releasing it. I've developed a small collection of special lures to entice a variety of fish, but, like Grandpa, I still prefer worms. Except I have to sneak into my wife's garden to avoid her warning to leave "her" worms alone. My favorite eating fish are *chaupukwi*, the native rainbow trout, and the German browns that were imported years ago.

So much was to be learned from Grandpa's and Grandpa John's

reminiscences of their fishing trips in the not-so-long-ago, when fishing was a family affair. The streams were filled with fish, they said. They always caught as much as they needed.

Men fished for suckers at night, when the fish were running in shallow water. They built fishing weirs, placing willow sticks strategically in the middle of the stream and swerving the weir toward shore. Fish were plentiful in the old days so it was easy to maneuver them. As they swam toward shore the men sometimes caught them by hand or speared them; women and children waited nearby to grab them as they were thrown to shore. After enough fish were caught the women put them in baskets and carried them either to a campsite, if they were on a several-day expedition, or home.

After the fish were cleaned some of them were baked for immediate eating. They were wrapped in leaves, laid in a shallow depression in the ground, and covered with soil. A fire was built over the depression; as it reduced to coals the fish baked slowly. Sometimes Grandma baked fish this way. It was delicious. The remaining fish were preserved for future meals; they were hung on poles or cords suspended between trees to air-dry. Dried fish were pounded apart and mixed with acorn flour into a meal, then formed into balls and eaten. Freezers now preserve whole fish for future meals.

One day when I was about seven or eight years old, the family drove down to Belleview Creek, a meandering stream through the foothills west of the road between O'Neal and Highway 145. Grandpa decided it was time for me to learn to fish the old way. He used chicken wire for the weir as it would have taken several hours to cut willow sticks. We waded into the stream, set up the weir, and in no time at all *kobodge* were swimming through it, toward shore. Some people call kobodge sucker or trash fish because they're considered unfit for food and are usually thrown away. We ate them because we didn't have much choice. They weren't that bad, after Grandma baked them over hot coals until they were so tender the meat flaked off.

Grandpa also showed me how to spear kobodge with a ten to fourteen-foot-long pole. First he speared one, then I tried. Then he speared another one, and I tried again. I finally gave up and joined Grandma, Mom, and Gloria, catching them by hand and throwing them on the bank. But Grandpa never gave up on me. On another trip I finally speared kobodge.

In the old days a spear shaft was made from straight branches of mountain mahogany or young bull pine trees. The point was made of obsidian that was grooved in the center and secured with pitch to the shaft. One end of a milkweed fiber thong was tied around the obsidian point so that by pulling the thong when the point entered the fish, the spearhead turned sideways, securing the spear. When I was a kid I watched Grandpa and Grandpa John make spear points out of ten to fourteen-inch-long, very slender pieces of hardwood. Or they'd strip metal bindings from crates and sharpen the metal into points. Then they'd attach the points to the poles with string made from milkweed or deer sinew so the point wouldn't break loose.

Grandpa also showed me how to catch *ebish*, a whitefish we sometimes called trash fish which swims in deep water. He'd stun them by throwing into the water the crushed leaves of turkey mullen that he'd gathered earlier. In the old days, when the stunned fish rose to the surface, women and children scooped them into baskets. We were alone, so we had to do it ourselves. Mom remembers stunning ebish when she and Grandma Daisy, Grandpa John's wife, used to fish in Whisky Creek. I don't like ebish; it has too many bones. But if it's baked a long time the bones fall off like salmon bones do and are soft enough to eat.

For some reason white people can't leave things alone. In the 1870s they began moving fish around. Jesse Ross hired some Indian women to catch trout from the San Joaquin River and plant them in Ross Creek. Two miners also caught a lot of fish from the river, but they didn't have the Indian women's talent; only three survived the journey to their transplanted home in Kaiser Creek.

In 1893 G. F. Hallock took fish from Ross Creek, descendants of the original transplants, and replanted them near the trail crossing at Fish Creek. In the early 1900s some fish journeyed by train from Colorado to be stocked at Rock Creek. By then no one knew what had happened to the originally stocked fish. In 1902 a recently built reservoir that impounded Willow Creek as it flowed through Crane Valley was planted with black bass. Crane Valley Reservoir was eventually renamed Bass Lake.

The old-timers fished year-round years ago, but their big fishing expeditions were for salmon, after they journeyed hundreds of miles from the Pacific Ocean up the San Joaquin River, surging against the swift-flowing water and cresting rapids and waterfalls to finally reach their old spawning grounds upriver from Cha:tiniu. There, Grandpa John reminisced, our ancestors speared salmon only a few hundred yards from the meadow where they lived.

Mom remembers that when she was a young girl living with her Grandma Lizzie at Peyakinu she would watch "Uncle Charlie and Uncle John taking off from home on their horses, riding over the ridges to the river near where Kerckhoff Dam is, to fish for salmon." Grandpa John, too, spoke animatedly of those days. I remember one day in particular, a few years before he died. We were sitting in Mom's kitchen when Grandpa described one of his salmon-fishing expeditions of years ago. After he and some of the other men reached the San Joaquin River, they awaited darkness. Then, torches lit, hands clasping their long poles, some of them stood on the bank while others waded into the river to stand on a boulder, waiting. As the salmon swam by they were attracted to the torchlight and swam toward it. Each man swiftly thrust his spear into the salmon. Grandpa John said they never missed. Lifting their spears overhead and backward, then thrusting forward, the Grandpas flung the speared salmon onto the bank, over and over again, until they had enough. They'd gather up the catch and return home.

In the old days there were two preferred fishing spots along the San Joaquin River: at Pakapanit, north of today's Italian Bar Road,

A young girl, Ethel Pomona, poses in the mid-1920s with part of her family's catch on the west bank of the San Joaquin River, above today's Redinger Dam. Her grandmother, Lizzie Capp Moore, is sitting on a granite boulder behind her and to her right. (Courtesy of Ethel Temple)

John Moore in the 1940s.
(Courtesy of Herb Punkin)

and at Samhau, near today's community of Chawanakee. Samhau was also a major crossing for Nɨm living on either side of the river, and where once, Grandpa said, Nɨm from the western side of the river retrieved from unapatɨ Nɨm from the eastern side of the river their stolen horses and women. Grandpa also liked to talk about a boyhood experience, when his father took him to Pasagɨ, near Chu:wani, where they stood on a large slick rock in the water and speared salmon, suckers, and trout.

Grandpa John also described a long-ago fishing trip. "Hotshot [Grandpa], Willie P. [Grandpa Willie], and John [their cousin, John Rogozinski] way down rock mountains, and then walked by river below Graveyard Meadow. Lots big salmon lay on sand waiting for trout to eat. Hungry." He said sometimes when they were fishing a "big snake come, big eyes, look at us. Old people say when he come to you give him fish to eat."

For eons past natural energy propelled the San Joaquin River westward. Through steep, narrow canyons, over and down rock falls, and into the San Joaquin Valley far below it rushed. Then, in the 1890s, John Eastwood was attracted to the high Sierra streams for their hydroelectric potential. He was the first of many to develop this energy source for the state's benefit. It did not benefit the Nim.

Initially, in 1896, Eastwood, as vice president, chief engineer, and superintendent of the San Joaquin Electric Company, developed a power house at what was still being described, erroneously, as the "north fork of the San Joaquin River" but was actually the separate drainage known today as Willow Creek. It was built just downstream from where my great-grandmother Kitty Camino Pomona's family was living. In 1901 Eastwood supervised the building of an earthen dam there. In 1910 it was enlarged with a second structure.

Pacific Light & Power Company, faced with the rapidly increasing population in southern California, was also attracted to the high Sierras. In 1910 and 1911 it acquired rights to develop the Big Creek Project, the first electric power project on the San Joaquin River. The salmon runs were doomed. Other projects eventually dammed Stevenson Creek, creating Huntington Lake and Shaver Lake reservoirs; Mono Creek, creating Lake Thomas A. Edison; and the south fork of the San Joaquin River, creating Florence Lake Reservoir. Our traditional river crossing at Yoninau disappeared. The earth-filled 330-foot high Mammoth Pool Reservoir was finished in 1959.

Still affected by the dam are descendants of the deer herd that was hunted by my ancestors. They are forced to swim across Mammoth Pool Reservoir during their June and September migrations. The U.S. Forest Service closes the reservoir to all activity during each migration to protect the deer from boaters and other intrusions. They claim that the deer are not stressed by their lengthy swim across the impounded water. My family knows otherwise.

Another power resource dam built on the San Joaquin River created Kerckhoff Lake. This dam destroyed the old-time river crossing at Chabodibau, where a bridge now links the communities of North Fork and Auberry.

Friant Dam, the westernmost major project on the middle fork of the San Joaquin River, located in the eastern San Joaquin Valley southeast of Clovis, became operational in the mid-twentieth century, when the federally sponsored Central Valley Project was completed. This dam provides irrigation water to farms in the central San Joaquin Valley. It also created Millerton Lake, which controls San Joaquin River floodwater. Buried beneath this artificial lake are Tomkit's encampment and the site of Camp Barbour. The government's failure to erect ladders on Friant Dam and others upriver prevented salmon from making their annual journey from the Pacific Ocean up the San Joaquin River to Cha:tiniu. The government also put a screen across Belleview Creek, where it empties into the San Joaquin River just below Friant Dam. This screen prevents kobodge from navigating upstream. All that remains are the reminiscences of my grandparents and those of other Nɨm families.

Grandma, too, watched for signs during puhiduwa. She'd listen for the song of a little gray bird I know only as *wishikojo*. Its sweet melody told her it was time to begin gathering food. Grandma was a skilled gatherer. So was Skunk.

Skunk and her children were hunting for food in the meadow. Her children were playing while she was gathering food. She was happy that she found all this food. She was singing, "Hei chau ka, hei chau pa, hei chau ka, hei chau pa, hei chau ka, hei chau pa, wi hi hiii wi hi hiii." Coyote heard this sound and went to see. He really was going to steal the food. He got to where Skunk was gathering food. "Oh, how pretty you look, Skunk." "Go on, leave us alone." But Coyote kept pestering Skunk. So she tired of this pest and she lifted her tail and sprayed Coyote. This is why Coyote smells like he does

when he gets wet. He pestered Skunk too long and now he remembers very well.   —as told by Grandma

Gathering is women's work; but because boys as well as girls were
with the women so much, they learned, too. Food gathering was a
communal activity. Some people gossiped while they worked; others could be heard singing; children tried to help but were usually
playing. No one ever thought that hunting, fishing, or food gathering was tedious and laborious, as many non-Indians believe. It's
what we do as families or several families together, Grandma said.
It is our way of life. My family continues to gather some of the
plants, and it's still fun.

The small bulbs of *ponowi,* one of the Brodiaea family, are dug
with a *poto,* a digging stick, before the plant flowers and are eaten
raw or boiled in water until soft. The long slender leaves of *wihi,*
one of many clovers that grow in our area, are also eaten raw. We
mix *pojida,* yet another clover, with *omagama.* Omagama is a salt
clover.

Before it flowers we eat the short, fragile stems of *pethis,* a wild
onion that grows in moist places. Pethis is delicious eaten wrapped
in a tortilla. Years ago Grandma transplanted a few of these plants
from another place to the creek bed a hundred feet behind our
home, where they have colonized and are a delightful addition to
our spring diet. A few years ago Mom gathered seed from Grandma's
planting and scattered it underneath a water spigot outside out
house. It grew there for several years.

Wild ginger sprouts are gathered in spring. We eat raw the short
fragile stems that are similar to the shallots available in markets. We
also dig ginger root and eat it raw or cooked in a broth. It can be
eaten year-round.

While walking we sometimes gently pull flowers from stems of
the manzanita tree. They're filled with sweet nectar. It's good. After
the flowers develop into green berries, we eat them, too.

In early spring we gather edible seeds from many wildflowers by "scooping" them into a gathering basket, woven into the shape of a cone with a handle made from split redbud bark. Seeds from the popcorn flowers are eaten raw. They taste even better after they're parched in a tightly woven basket capable of holding the seeds mixed with hot coals. The basket is shaken vigorously until the coals drop out. Since Grandma died, though, we seldom gather flower seeds.

At about midspring we used to gather and eat raw the *tupigini* that grows wild in rock crevices near creeks. Tupigini looks like the garden succulent known as hens and chicks.

Many plants are still gathered in late spring. The tubers of the Mariposa lily are dried after they are dug up, and then boiled. Roots of *tena,* a plant with yellow flowers, are also dug and eaten raw. So are wild carrot tubers, but they can also be dried or boiled. We gather watercress from streams and eat it raw or boiled; sometimes we fry it in meat fat. The green leaves of a plant we call *wadzaki* are boiled and dipped into manzanita berry juice; then they're eaten. We also eat raw wild strawberries and ground cherries. I've heard that ground cherries may have been introduced to our area during pioneer cattle drives,

We used to gather *sagwanoi,* a caterpillar worm that resembles the tomato worm. It lives on the flower Farewell to Spring. Mom says you first "squeezed the innards out of the worm and baked it on hot rocks or dried the worm and then boiled it." We don't eat them anymore.

After the winter rains we begin gathering most of the mushrooms. Mushrooms are one of the few foods my family still gathers annually. Many non-Indians are afraid of mushrooms because some varieties are poisonous, but as Mom says, "We know what to pick and when to pick. Someone else would go up and not know and could get sick." It's on her advice that I'm not identifying some of the mushrooms.

We gather many different kinds, to be eaten raw, pan-fried in bacon grease, as we usually do now, or cooked into a delicious broth by Mom, who learned this method from her Grandma Lizzie. Some mushrooms can be air-dried for later use as well as eaten raw or freshly cooked. Other mushrooms can't be dried and must be eaten within twenty-four hours.

In the old days women knew it was time to gather mushrooms when oak leaves began sprouting. Many newcomers to the area bemoan the foggy days that accompany spring, when the clear early morning sunlight suddenly disappears as the fog lifts itself into the mountains. We welcome the fog, whose presence is necessary for some of the mushroom crop to grow.

Several mushroom varieties are gathered in late spring. The bolita mushroom can be eaten raw. It's also boiled, and is really good fried in bacon grease or made into mushroom gravy. But it must be used within hours after it is gathered. The morel, which grows at elevations above 5,000 feet, and profusely after a fire, is boiled into a soup. It can also be dried.

Mom says Grandpa John was our only contemporary family member who liked to eat *pagu*, a toadstool that grows at lower elevations. "My aunts ate it, too," she says. Pagu, which can't be dried, is picked while young and firm, then boiled until soft. The coral mushroom is also gathered in spring. It can be either dried or boiled until soft and then eaten.

No mushrooms are gathered during the hot days of summer.

When it's cold and wet, from November through January, we gather *sekayu*, the fairy ring mushroom. If winter temperatures are mild, sometimes this mushroom doesn't appear until early spring. Regardless, it only appears in a wet year. I think sekayu is the best of all the mushrooms. These days we sometimes gather it near Pogoya, which is near Fish Creek Mountain. It's delicious eaten freshly fried or boiled into a broth. Since we pick so many at a time, it's also air-dried and then stored. Whenever we're hungry for sekayu, we can cook it into a broth or add it to other recipes.

In the late winter of 1993, after it had rained for days, a bunch of the family drove to Pogoya and had a great day gathering sekayu.

It had been a long time since the family had been all together, gathering mushrooms. I'm sure each of us was aware of Grandma's and Grandpa's absence. We estimated that altogether we gathered eighty pounds of fresh mushrooms. That sounds like a lot, but after Mom and my wife, Judy, dried the bulk of them the amount was greatly reduced. There were still plenty to last a long time, though, and to share with others.

No'i appears on black oaks after the first fall rain. If cooked fresh, no'i must be boiled for a long time, or you get sick. One time I forgot to cook no'i and ate it raw. It turned my guts inside out. No'i can also be dried.

Several other mushroom varieties are gathered in late winter. *Yapina* grows on willow trees that flourish along creek beds; it's cooked the same way as the fairy ring mushroom. *Naka* is boiled and often mixed up with other mushrooms. Yapina and naka can also be dried. *Tastu,* not a well-known mushroom, can't be dried; it is always boiled before eating.

When I drive past the many places I went to with Grandma as a child, I still search for rows of white mushroom caps beneath the trees. Or I seek mushrooms in the bulging pine needles on the ground, or watch for a yellow splotch of color on the trunks of oaks.

Pogoya is also a good place to gather *tuna,* bull pine nuts. Late spring is the best time to eat them, when they are still green and soft. The young nut is best. We always eat them raw. By late summer tuna are so hard they're difficult to crack, even with a rock. The nut is removed from the burr by hitting each section with a sharp rock. By rubbing the cone's core in our hands, we easily remove the pitch that sticks to them. The burr is placed between the teeth, the same as an artichoke leaf, and the nut is easily scraped off into the mouth.

When we gathered pine nuts when I was little Grandpa usually told us about the adventures of Squirrel and Opossum. The piles of stripped pine cones laying at the base of pine trees, he said, were left by Squirrel, who also knows how to get to the nuts.

Squirrel and Opossum were sitting on a limb in the afternoon. Squirrel was cracking bull pine nuts for Opossum. Opossum can't see in daylight so Squirrel was giving the dead ones to Opossum. All the time Squirrel was singing:

> Mai tila wai gan gan
> Mai tila wai gan gan
> Mai tila wai gan gan
> Mai tila wai gan gan.
> Hu ju ju ju.

He was distracting Opossum so he wouldn't know he was getting dead nuts.

Grandpa would then remind us, "Don't be half asleep or someone will trick you."

In late spring, usually in May, we used to gather *huya,* the pupa stage of a butterfly caterpillar, probably the California tortoise-shell. When we saw thousands of this butterfly species flying around, we knew they were ready to metamorphose into the pupa stage. The pupae hang from chaparral bushes before they emerge as caterpillars. Huya gorge themselves in a frenzy of feasting, stripping the chaparral leaves off the branches. We'd call to them, "Hoo, hoo," and they'd answer by shaking themselves. So we knew where to go to gather the huya, by the bucketful. It took several days to gather a large enough supply.

Grandma cleaned and washed the huya and then put them into a wet gunnysack. She put the sack on a bed of coals in a sunken pit, covered the pit with dirt, and roasted them overnight. In the morning she took the huya out of the sack and air-dried them. Then she cooked them in a pot, with a small amount of water, until the water cooked down, just like cooking beans. It's delicious! Mom, who really enjoys huya, says, "They have nice, real orange-colored juice to them. They're tasty!"

In the old days huya was cooked in baskets filled with water and heated with hot rocks. Sometimes they were roasted, wrapped in sacks women wove with ferns, probably the Woodwardia, or they wrapped the huya in leaves or cut grass. "I never did ask my Grandmother about that," Mom said, "We didn't ask questions in those days." The last time my family ate huya was in the 1970s. They are supposed to return every ten years or so, but we haven't seen them since then.

Salt is available from several sources. It appears naturally on the *omagama,* the salty-tasting clover that grows in damp places in the mountains. Salt falls right off the omagama when it's dried. It, too, is eaten raw. We used to drive up to a meadow at Hoyakwe, now the community of Cascadel, a few miles above our home to gather omagama. It has virtually disappeared from there because of increasing land development.

The Nɨm used to trade for salt grass with the Komotini, our name for all Indians living in the San Joaquin Valley, or with Indians east of the Sierra Nevada, who collected raw salt from dry lake beds during summer.

During puhiduwa, as in other seasons throughout the year, a number of other plants were used. Bark stripped from branches of the flannel bush was used for straps to carry loads, especially firewood. These loads were carried on the back with a tump line fashioned from finger-woven milkweed fibers which was tied to the load and supported at the forehead. Some straps were also made from a plant we call *pabu.*

Leaves from the bay tree were laid over the hot rocks in the sweathouse. When water was poured on the rocks to create steam, a pungent and soothing fragrance filled the structure.

Pitch from the yellow and bull pine trees and the incense cedar tree was medicine: applied to a skin wound it sealed the wound, just like a bandage. Yellow pine pitch was also chewed, like gum. Grandpa John said milkweed was, too, in the old days.

Mom still forms spoons from bull pine saplings and uses them to stir acorn during the cooking process. She also still makes sticks from branches of young incense cedars, to pick up the hot rocks used in cooking acorn and in the sweathouse.

Grandma said it was fun living in the old days, when she was young. Her grandma described how even the San Joaquin River, swollen with springtime's heavy rain and melting snow, didn't stop people who lived west of the river from traveling to the other side, to hot springs or to visit family and friends over there. During winter and spring a grapevine cable was carried across the river by a swimming man and then stretched high above the flowing water, from one tree to another. George A. Dorsey described how the Indians crossed "by means of a cable made from the bark of the Fremontii Californica tree, stretched just above the water, and along which they cl[u]ng and pull[ed] themselves across."[1] They were aided by a rope fastened to their bodies that was tugged on by people who'd already crossed. In summer and fall the water was low enough so that people crossed over on a footbridge made with live oak limbs that were tied together.

Dorsey reported that at the turn of the century travelers crossed the San Joaquin River on a wooden bridge "held up by four great chains anchored to either bank." He continued, "Like many other rivers . . . crossings are difficult because of the extreme depth and the swiftness of the current, thus rendering boats and ferries impracticable, while bridges are rare."[2]

Ogi, big time celebrations, were held at several places in the Sierra Nevada. Grandma said they were at Soyakinu, Kinsman Flat; at Yauwatinyu, a spring near Willow Creek; at Chu:wani, a flat place east of the San Joaquin River; at Muchipi, the North Fork Recreation Center; at Pagasanina, a locale below the Hogue Ranch; at Yowinau, the Rex Ranch on Road 222; and at Cha:tiniu. She said tribal leaders from east of the Sierra Nevada often came to the ogi.

An ogi was a time to sit back and relax. Since smoking was a social activity, not intended for ceremonies or blessings, people relaxed by smoking the crushed leaves of our native tobacco plant in a to´ish. There wasn't any narcotic effect, Grandma said. Our family made the to´ish by rolling red clay, found throughout our area, into a fat tube and squeezing it into shape by hand. The tube was hollowed out by inserting a finger into it. The pipe was air-dried until it was hard enough for a good smoke. Kids today learn how to make similar pipes in kindergarten. We didn't know about the "peace pipe" until we started watching movies.

Card games have replaced stick gambling. Grandma often took Gloria and me with her on weekends when she'd play cards for hours with her lady friends. We often went to Coarsegold where she had many friends after her marriage to Jim Bobb, a Wowa from there. Mom drove. Old Lady Poker, sometimes called Indian Poker, is still a favorite card game. It's wild! While the ladies played cards, we kids played outside until we were so exhausted we finally fell asleep.

Handgames are games of chance that pit teams from different tribes against each other. Many Indians still play handgames, but Mom says they haven't been played much in our territory since she was a girl in the late 1920s. "The Chukchansi at Coarsegold played them a lot," she says. Grandma taught me how to play, and I sometimes played on a team with her and Grandpa Willie.

Each handgame team is composed of five or more people (men and women play together) sitting in a line facing each other and separated by a few feet. Bets are placed ahead of time. Today we use money, but years ago people bet furs and baskets and, after their arrival, horses. My family used to play with ten sticks and two pairs of bones fashioned from the forearms of a mountain lion.

The game's purpose is for the opposing team to guess which two people on the opposite team hold the bones and in which hand. If they guess correctly, they win that set of sticks, continuing to guess until one team possesses all of them. The game can last a half hour, an hour, two hours, even all night, and isn't over until one team holds all ten counting sticks.

Handgames require attention. Throughout the game the opposing teams are not just trying to win sticks by guessing who has the

Left to right: Margaret Moore Bobb, Willie Pomona, Henry Jones, Jr., Rosalie Bethel, Raleigh Jones, and an unidentified boy with his back to the camera. They are playing a handgame at the North Fork Recreation Center in 1973. (Courtesy of Vivian Kneppel)

bones, but the players are constantly intimidating each other with handgame songs and mind tricks. Some people "own" their songs or, with permission, sing the songs of others.

The singing is usually accompanied by some team members holding clappers. The clappers are made from an elderberry tree branch. Bark is stripped from a slender twelve-inch or so branch, and then the branch is split three quarters of the way down and the pith is removed. The clapping sound is achieved by holding the clapper in one hand and hitting it on the palm of the other. Many people now just hit a log with a stick.

Songs have great power and can upset an opposing team. Watch the eyes, Grandpa Willie said. They give people away. Tease the other team. They become aggravated. And give clues to help you win. The winning team is usually composed of players with the more powerful mind tricks and songs and the greater ability to intimidate.

There's a great story about handgames.

The Nɨm gathered at a house called Mus. They had challenged each other to play handgames. A young woman was menstruating and was not let inside the house. She was covered by a *wono* [a burden basket] and tied down with a stick at the outside of the entrance. The handgame was going strong well into midnight. The young woman heard a sound coming from the mountainside. "Wemu, wemu, wemu." She heard this and called out from under the wono, "Something is coming. I hear it." The people inside just said, "It's only your shit saying that," and kept on gambling. The sound came closer and closer, "Wemu, wemu, wemu." The woman asked them to stop and the same reply came, "It's only your shit. Don't bother us. We are going strong." One woman had a baby and was breastfeeding it. Wemu got to Mus and walked in. All the players looked at him and all froze in the positions they were in. Some were showing their handgame bones, some were hiding bones behind their backs. They all froze with their eyes open except for the baby who was suckling its mother. Then the Wemu left, and as he was leaving he tried to lift the wono up where the woman was. He tried, but couldn't lift it off. The baby was crying loud. The woman heard the sound and came out from under the wono. She said, "Come with me and I will feed you. I will dig *ponowi, kipiha,* and *tena.*" She took the child and fed and raised her.

Grandma always warned us after she told this story, "Don't tease people when they are telling the truth. If you do, you will turn to stone."

The wemu Grandma described isn't a fairy-tale character. He is real, a choap, a ghost, with red eyes. The wemu carries a wono on his back in which he has a spike that he uses to impale babies so he can eat them. I remember one night, after Grandma opened the

Willie Pomona in about 1915,
dressed like his hero, the
Hollywood star Tom Mix.
(Author's collection)

door when we returned home from the show, she noticed a really
bad smell inside. "The wemu has been here," she said. One day, in
the 1960s, Grandpa told us he'd smelled the wemu over several
nights, when it visited him after he was in bed.

Footracing was popular. Men ran for many miles, up and down
the hills, competing against each other. My uncles, Harvey and
Herb, ran over our property a lot when they were boys. They even
ran up the trees. The lower branches of some of the pines are still
bent down because of the weight placed on them years ago.

A summertime rodeo at the Crane Valley meadow in the early 1900s. This locale, in the western portion of the meadow, is now covered by Bass Lake. (Author's collection)

Both men and women played shinny, separating into teams of several people. A ball made from knots off an oak tree was hit with a stick, back and forth, sometimes for miles, Grandpa said, until one team won.

Two people could play a game with a bead (replaced in recent years with a button). It was put on a length of string. Each contestant held an end of the string and began twirling the bead. The winner was the one who kept the bead twirling the longest.

Indian rodeos and horse races were held in spring, through summer, and into fall. There was a big rodeo at Pauha, a meadow now covered with water at the north end of Bass Lake. Spectators stood shoulder to shoulder in a circle that formed a human fence, as the mounted contestants performed their feats of daring on wild, bucking horses. Unlike the white man's rodeo of several events, Nɨm rodeos had only the bucking horse event.

Grandpa competed at Pauha. I've been told by other family

members that he was quite a rider, one of the best, dressed in cuffed Levis, a cowboy shirt, boots, and his black felt hat. Even when he quit riding horses he dressed the same way for years afterward. That was all before my time. Remnants of barbed-wire that once surrounded our property to corral Grandpa's horses are still visible. When they were young Grandpa John and Grandpa Willie also competed often.

Rodeos, horse races, and footraces were also held "where Little Jim and Big Jim lived at Muchipi," Grandpa said, where the North Fork Recreation Center is today. Rodeos were also held at two places called Naboyoha, meaning "racing." One is just west of today's Road 274, above the county dump; the other is just east of Road 200, at the westerly boundary of North Fork.

All of these joyful occasions began to disappear with the dawn of the twentieth century, as racial prejudice and Christian church influence intruded on our culture. Federal authorities stopped us from using Sierra National Forest land, and settlers homesteaded other land.

But a few years ago I glimpsed what it was like in the past, while attending a powwow at Carson City, Nevada, where Indian dancers from throughout the Great Basin area competed in modern intertribal competition. A bright desert sun warmed the lazy afternoon. There was a lull in the competition. An older man entered the arena and began singing, accompanying himself as he beat steadily on a hand-drum, an uncommon instrument at modern powwows. Scores of spectators, Judy and I included, jumped to their feet, beckoned by the old songs of a *nïgaba,* a social round dance. Everyone hurried into the arena to join in the fast-paced dance that continued for several minutes. As quickly as it began, it ended.

All cultures share the problems of guiding boys and girls into adolescence when they are attracted each to the other. This happened often at celebrations or rodeos, Grandma fondly recalled, but she said parents usually kept a tight rein on their pubescent children.

Our language has no word to describe either love or its emotion.

Charlie "Hotshot" Moore at Peyakinu in 1919. In his younger days he usually dressed like his hero, the Hollywood cowboy star Tom Mix. (Author's collection)

Instead we were taught to care for and share with one another. Marriages were arranged by parents. It wasn't necessarily required to marry within one's side or clan, although my family tried to, but it was absolutely prohibited to marry a relative, no matter how distant the relationship was. Even today our family alerts its youth; there's always someone who is well versed in our genealogy.

My maternal grandmother, Emma Moore, was the last of our family and one of the last women of our tribe whose marriage, in the early 1920s, was arranged. When children were shrouded in the bosom of the family, before the influences of the non-Indian culture affected them, traditions were accepted without question. Grandma Emma had no voice in the decision.

Dick and Kitty Pomona sent word to Emma's parents, Jim and Lizzie Moore, that they wanted their son, Willie, to marry Emma.

Willie and Emma Moore Pomona at Mentone during a summer grape harvest in the early 1920s. (Author's collection)

On a prearranged day the Pomonas, who lived southwest of North Fork near the main road to the San Joaquin Valley, came to the Moores' house at Peyakinu with the bridal price of horses and baskets. The arrangement was sealed after both families drank acorn from a basket specially woven for the occasion. Emma Moore and Willie Pomona were married.

Mom remembers that in her childhood her father and her maternal grandmother never spoke to each other. It was during my grandparents' generation that the custom of a man or wife not speaking to their in-laws disappeared. Neither spouse was permitted to talk to the in-law of the opposite sex but could convey messages through a third party. Communication with the in-law of the same sex was not prohibited. The reason for this custom disappeared long before the custom itself, but I believe it was a form of respect toward the parents-in-law.

In the old days childbearing was a natural result of marriage. Because the extended family lived in close proximity to each other, they were all involved in raising a child. Grandma and Grandpa helped Mom raise Gloria and me after Mom went to work. Our extended family preserved the Nɨm lifestyle for us.

Family size was limited to two or three children, Grandma said. People knew intuitively nature's ability to sustain life and never taxed the land. Women knew how to control or abort birth by using specific plants, Grandma said.

In the early years of this century many Nɨm families were unable to resist white people's pressure to conform to their culture. Some families stopped speaking the Nɨm language, and customs and traditions were lost. Fortunately, Grandpa and Grandma continued to speak the old language. I learned it from them and spoke only Nɨm with them. More fortunate still, Mom spoke to Gloria and me in English, so that when I began elementary school in the mid-1950s I was already bilingual.

In retrospect, I think the most important lesson Grandma taught me was respect. She counseled respect for ourselves, for others, for all life, no matter what its form. When you respect with sincerity, from the heart, she said, then you travel through life without offending anything or anyone, and life is easier and simpler.

All children test their parents. I tested Mom and my grandparents, but I don't recall they ever spanked me much. Rather, if I was disobedient, the greater punishment was my own shame, that in some way I had humiliated them.

We were taught to not ask too many questions but to listen and follow by example. We seemed to know inherently that at the right time we would learn what we needed. I was aware, though, that we would be sent out to play when others came to visit. "Little pitchers have big ears" may be a non-Indian phrase, but my grandparents and Mom practiced the same idea.

CHAPTER SEVEN

WHEN THE GRASS IS DRYING UP

My grandparents called summer *tazewano,* "when the grass is drying up." Grandma said the drying grass told women to begin filling baskets with dried fish and meat, springtime seeds, and preserved mushrooms. Acorns, too, were packed into baskets, unless the family was returning to the previous year's summer place where the nuts had been cached before they returned to their winter home. The day finally came when the baskets were settled on the women's backs, the children were hustled together, and everyone walked to the higher, cooler elevations of the Sierra Nevada, walking, that is, until horses were acquired.

Beneath tall stands of pines at the edge of meadows, where tall grass waved in the mountain breeze, my ancestors erected new tonobi and sweathouses if those from the previous summer were not suitable. Arbors were built, too, of strong live oak limbs to hold the framework of smaller branches. Because their dried leaves seldom fall, small branches from bay or willow trees were the preferred wood to layer across the top of the framework, the dense mat of leaves providing shade during tazewano's bright sunny days. The fragrant bay leaves, especially, repelled pesky insects.

Food was plentiful. The men hunted deer, squirrel, and rabbit.

They also fished streams and lakes. Stream fishing was still done at night with the weir and spear, but at this elevation they caught chaupukwi, the rainbow trout. It is absolutely delicious when baked fresh. If chaupukwi is dried, the meat has to be boiled to eat. Lake fishing was done during the day. A man stood on a raft, armed with a spear, waiting for his quarry. Rafts were easily constructed with tule grass that grows abundantly on the shores of high Sierra lakes.

When Mom was a little girl she glimpsed what tazewano meant to our ancestors. Her grandparents, Jim and Lizzie Moore, took the family to Granite Creek for two leisurely weeks of camping and fishing. Grandpa Jim, his sons, and the women, too, panned the creek for gold, she remembers, usually finding enough to make the trip profitable as well as pleasurable. Later, when they returned to their home at Peyakinu, they'd travel in a horse-drawn wagon into North Fork to buy supplies.

The San Joaquin River was never far from any place my ancestors lived, winter or summer. During tazewano they took clams from the river. "You would dive in for them, make a fire and throw them on it," Mom said, "which was the only way you could get the meat. Then you'd eat them. I never ate them. I didn't care for them."

Blackberries and strawberries were sweet treats. Mouth-puckering fruit from the sourberry bush was everywhere. Sourberries are bright red when they've ripened in midsummer, and sticky from their own natural "salt." We still enjoy gathering berries each summer.

In the summer of 1992 Grandpa John and Grandma Daisy were eager to pick sourberries, so we arranged a family outing. They wore us out! Mom, her grandson, Jimmy Jeff, the grandparents, and Judy and I left home about 9 o'clock for what I expected would be a short morning. We picked berries until 1 o'clock, traveling from place to place until we had many bags full, plus all the berries we ate as we picked!

Many non-Indians screw up their faces when they eat this berry because it is so sour, but we relish them, usually mashing them,

John Moore picking
sourberries in the summer
of 1992 near North Fork.
(Author's collection)

adding fresh salt and a little water, and digging in. You have to be
careful not to eat too many at one time, though, as sourberries can
cause diarrhea.

One day, while we were walking on our property, Mom demon-
strated how in the old days if you were out and about and came
upon a sourberry bush but didn't have a basket to carry the berries
in, you could make a sack. She bent down and plucked large
leaves from the mullein plant and wove a pouch with twigs she
picked up from the ground. This pouch, she said, was used only
to collect sourberries.

Because the gooseberry has spiny flesh, the women used a stick
to knock them from bush to basket and then rubbed them gently
with a rock, an easy way to remove the spines without being stuck.
Mom still gathers gooseberries this way. They're eaten raw but can
be dried for later use.

Elderberries are also eaten, raw or dried. Although these bushes grow in the foothills, we prefer the elderberries that grow at the higher elevations.

When I was a kid I had great fun playing games with the other children while the adults gathered elderberries. Grandpa taught me how to make a popgun from elderberry wood. You first poke out the soft pith with a stick. Ripe serviceberries are ammunition. A berry is put into both ends of the hollow wood, and when a stick is shoved into one end the berries are pushed out the other, striking one's "enemy." I can't wait to teach my young grandchild, Anthony, how to play.

Grandpa also taught me another game during tazewano. When the buckeye trees have finished flowering and their chestnut-size nuts appear at the ends of limbs, I'd clamber into a tree to break limbs off the main branch. They were great weapons when playing "cowboys and Indians." By holding the limb behind one's shoulder and flicking it quickly overhead, the nuts broke free and flew toward the "enemy." They hurt! Of course, the Indians always won.

We still make juice from berries gathered from the manzanita. They are usually ready in early August. Taste-testing determines when they're very sweet and ready for picking.

Nowadays we handpick the ripe berries into a pail or basket. In the old days women cleared the ground of duff and trash and knocked the berries off with a stick, Mom says, collecting them from the ground into burden baskets. After the berries were washed and crushed they were shaped into a cone on a loosely woven flat basket that was set on top of a tightly woven waterproof basket. Water was periodically drizzled over the berries for several hours to collect their flavor as the water dripped downward. "You just know when the juice is ready," Mom says. "It tastes very sweet." Cheesecloth has replaced the loosely woven basket, and a bowl the watertight basket. Otherwise, the method is the same. Manzanita berries are also eaten raw and the spring-blooming flower has a delicate, sweet flavor.

Ethel Pomona Temple
making manzanita
berry juice in 1994,
during a demonstration
at the California Basket-
weavers Conference at the
Miwok Rancheria near
Tuolumne, California. She
is holding a winnowing
basket filled with berries.
(Courtesy of Ethel Temple)

Instead of the mountain mahogany, manzanita branches were sometimes used for walking sticks. And because manzanita wood makes a very hot fire, it was burned to heat the soapstone rocks used when cooking acorn.

Chinquapin and hazelnuts were also gathered during tazewano. The dry seeds of *chat,* a wildflower known as chia, are still gathered, soon after the days become hot. We pick the flower stalks and shake the dried heads into a pail. In the old days the seeds were gathered in a basket that had a woven handle and gently bent sides so it looked like a scoop. The seeds are still pounded in a mortar, mixed with manzanita juice into about a one-inch-diameter ball, and then eaten.

Another food gathered by women during their mountain stay was *sitin,* a very pungent green onion. It's eaten raw. We still pull it up if we're in the mountains. It's delicious, whether wrapped in a tortilla, spread on greasebread, or cooked into a gravy.

I've never eaten *piyag,* the caterpillar that metamorphoses into the Pandora moth, but Grandma said it is a delicacy. Toward the end of tazewano the piyag crawl down the trunks of the Ponderosa pines, to burrow in the soil for the winter. During that season they form pupal cases from which Pandora moths emerge the next summer.

When the old-timers saw piyag crawling down the trunk after gorging themselves on pine needles, they dug a shallow trench with sloping sides. The piyag were trapped and easily gathered. After the intestines were cleaned out the piyag were roasted by combining them with hot coals in a winnowing basket and shaking the basket vigorously until they were cooked. Or, Grandma said, the piyag could be thrown directly onto the hot coals left in a fire pit. Piyag can also be dried and stored for later eating.

When the milkweed plant dried and became brittle it was gathered to manufacture string. Grandma showed me how to bunch together lengths of fiber and roll them by hand on my thigh so they bound together tightly. She combed the soft strands with a stick to smooth the lengths and to remove loose string. In the old days, milkweed was used to string bows, for fishing line, and to secure a breakaway obsidian or bone point to a spear, enabling a hunter to retrieve the point when it struck fish. It was also woven into tump lines worn across the forehead, each end of which was tied to a load carried on the back.

Ceremonial singers once wore belts made with woven milkweed string, onto which they'd secure woodpecker scalps, yellow hummingbird feathers, and white shell beads. Some singers still wear belts, but they are usually woven with colored yarn that was substituted for milkweed when it became available in the early 1900s. It was also about then that the ceremonial singers stopped using woodpecker scalps and feathers, to avoid being maligned and chastised by Christian missionaries, although for a while they continued to use the white beads. Mom weaves yarn belts to sell; they have fanciful designs in a variety of colors. I treasure Grandma's belt, which she wove with scores of minuscule red and white beads on fine string. She gave it to me before she died.

During tazewano, as at puhiduwa, families from throughout the mountain camps gathered to feast, gossip, and play games. But as white people increasingly moved into the foothills and mountains, these pleasant days gradually ended.

CHAPTER EIGHT

THE WARM DAYS
OF SUMMER BRING
SETTLERS

The seasons came and went. Because they still lived in isolated locales, my ancestors seldom saw outsiders. But as settlers continued to move into the central Sierra Nevada foothills and mountains, the family's activities during tazewano gradually changed. And political events at the state and federal level were taking place which would disrupt their lifestyle even more.

Settlers successfully lobbied the state legislature in April 1856 to create Fresno County from land in the once-immense Mariposa County and from smaller parts of Merced and Tulare counties. My family was still living at Cha:tiniu in May 1859 when surveyors, hired by the federal government, plotted the first maps of the higher elevations of the Sierra Nevada west of the San Joaquin River. One surveyor noted that the land was especially good for summer grazing.

A lack of roads in the early 1860s didn't stop ranchers in the San Joaquin Valley and lower Sierra Nevada foothills from driving their stock along Indian trails into the high Sierras each summer. There they competed with Nɨm families who still lived around the meadows where the cattle grazed. The ranchers won.

In 1854 a wagon road was built from Fort Miller to Crane Valley, and a sawmill was soon opened there. Another crude road was extended in 1865, from Crane Valley to a small community that was developing just west of what was described as the north fork of the San Joaquin. At the end of that road Milton Brown built a log cabin, thought by local historians to be the first house in the area. Brown began to sell supplies from his home to stockmen, sheepmen, and miners, who left their wagons with him while they packed supplies and drove stock higher into the mountains, even as far as Cha:tiniu.

At first the packers called the area around Brown's store "Brown's place," but as a small settlement grew around the store settlers called the area North Fork, because of its location next to what was then believed to be the north fork of the San Joaquin River. The Nɨm called that location wa´ap, as the area was then covered with cedars. It didn't take long for settlers to cut down most of the cedars for wood to build their homes and fences. Brown's log cabin and most of the cedars are gone.

By 1877 the road from "Brown's place" had been extended eastward several miles to what became known as Cascadel. Another small store opened near Alder Creek, not far from our present home, where a few groceries, calico cloth, and whiskey was sold. Local folklore suggests it was the sale of whiskey that influenced someone to change the creek's name from Alder to Whisky. It's still called that.

Brown also introduced hogs to the area, grazing them at Brown's Meadow near Shuteye Mountain. Each fall he and several other ranchers drove combined herds of up to one thousand head from North Fork to the Stockton market, assisted by Nɨm men they had hired. The drive usually took about two months, but when a railroad through the San Joaquin Valley was opened in 1875 the time was shortened by driving the hogs to the railhead near Fresno.

Great-grandpa Jim raised hogs around the turn of the century. Grandpa said his dad told him that one day "they" came and took them. During this period the federal government was indiscriminately rounding up all the hogs in the forest, claiming the animals caused too much trouble running loose and eating anything and everything. So the government hired a local man to buy all the hogs at a low price and drive them to valley markets in herds of four hundred to five hundred. Grandpa said the government never paid his dad.

Brown also planted grain southwest of North Fork, near Fish Creek Mountain. He'd harvest it each summer with the help of about fifty Nɨm women. Some of Mom's paternal family who lived near there went to work for him. Mothers hung their babies in baskets from the limbs of oaks while they worked. Each baby was wrapped in a rabbit skin blanket and secured in the basket with deerskin bindings. They slept snugly in the trees as their mothers worked.

The women cut the heads off the grain and put them into baskets hung on their backs. After they dumped their loads on the ground, Brown drove horses over and over the grain until it was threshed. Then, using winnowing baskets, the women tossed the threshed grain into the air; the wind blew the chaff away as the grain fell back into their baskets. The women were paid in grain, which they carried home in their burden baskets.

Diets slowly changed. Grandma said that as her grandparents saw the vegetables that the settlers planted in their gardens, they, too, began to plant vegetable gardens. They also began to supplement their traditional diet of deer meat with beef from the few cows or steers they obtained from their white neighbors.

Even though the Nɨm were influenced to adapt to some of the white men's ways, they continued to struggle with change. As their culture was bombarded by new ideas introduced by the settlers and as they saw their land taken from them, their food supplies diminish, and new diseases cause illness and death because they lacked resistance to them, many Nɨm were ready when a new religion was shared with them.

After Tavibo, a Paiute chief and medicine man from the Great Basin area east of the Sierra Nevada, began describing his visions, the Ghost Dance religion, as it was described, flourished and spread. This religion combined old Indian ideas and new Christian beliefs, stressing rules of conduct that would persuade the father, the world's creator, to return to earth, bringing with him everyone who had died.

Wovoka, who was also known as Jack Wilson, was related to Tavibo. Soon he, too, was preaching the Ghost Dance message; he also claimed that white people would disappear and the Indians would regain peace and prosperity.

The Ghost Dance religion was introduced to the Nɨm by an unidentified Paiute man who was one of Wovoka's missionaries. He arrived at a Nɨm encampment near the San Joaquin River in 1870, where he met Joijoi, who may have been a leader. If he was, Joijoi's conversion would have been of great benefit to the missionary.

Joijoi arranged for the first Ghost Dance to be held at Saganu, a settlement west of Kana´au, in May 1870. Messages of invitation were sent to Nɨm living in other areas and to San Joaquin Valley Indians to join the Saganu residents at the dance.

Chinitit's family, who may still have been living at Cha:tiniu, probably heard about the gathering. But Grandma said she didn't know if they ever went to a Ghost Dance. "Somebody came over from Bishop a long time ago," Grandma recalled. "He was teaching a new religion, but they [the Nɨm] didn't take it."

By dancing and the verbal repetition of prayers of petition, a foreign concept that was taught to the people by the missionary, they believed that they could envision the rebirth of all who had died. As the singers sat inside a dance circle, adorned with feather headdresses and accompanying themselves with handclappers, others performed a dance that is similar to the nɨgabɨ, the vigorous dance we enjoyed at the Carson City powwow. The people danced on six consecutive nights, from dark until midnight, after which everyone slept.

When white settlers in the area heard about this new Indian "religion" that taught, among other things, that they would disappear, fear spread by word of mouth that an Indian uprising was imminent. The August 24, 1870, issue of the *Fresno Weekly Expositor* cautioned against retaliation and pleaded the Indians' cause:

> For several days past rumors have been flying about that the Fresno and Mono Indians, assisted by the Pah Utes, were about to commence hostilities against the whites. . . . The Indians have many grievances to complain of, and that they should be incited to seek revenge does not seem improbable. They depend, in a great measure, for their sustenance upon the grass, seeds and acorns, which they gather in the mountains. This season cattle and hogs have been driven thither in great numbers, and as a consequence they have been robbed of their grass seeds and acorns. In some instances, we are told, white men have forbidden them, under any circumstances, gathering acorns at different points in the mountains, as they wished to keep them to feed their hogs upon. Some Indians had small gardens of corn and melons, these were broken into by cattle and hogs and completely destroyed, so naturally enough the "poor Lo's," seeing starvation staring them in the face, have undoubtedly made some harsh threats.[1]

The reporter also suggested that settlers take precautions against possible attack, as his paper learned that some of the Indian encampments had been abandoned.

Within just a few days fifty settlers and a large number of Indians met at Baseau's Store, northeast of Crane Valley, to discuss the feared uprising. The *Fresno Weekly Expositor* reported this meeting on September 7, 1870:

> The principal Indian Chiefs, of the tribes which reside in that section, . . . stated that they had never contemplated any difficulty with the whites; that while their gardens had been destroyed by the stock, and other wrongs had been inflicted upon them, they preferred to suffer rather than raise a difficulty, and that they wanted

peace, but should other Indians see fit to raise a fight they would stand by the whites.[2]

The meeting ended, according to the article, with the settlers deciding "that there is not a particle of danger of any trouble, and that the reports were gotten up by the parties who had stock in the mountains, with a view to frighten away others, so that they might have more pasture room."[3]

Less than a month later, settlers east of the San Joaquin River feared an uprising above "Humphrey & Mock's mill," where Meadow Lakes Basin is today. Although forty to fifty men were organized to chastise the mountain Indians, apparently nothing developed, and the fear of uprisings receded.

About five hundred Indians attended another Ghost Dance gathering at Eshom Valley in the San Joaquin Valley, east of the present-day community of Badger. On the sixth night of continuous dancing there was a horse dance, with mounted Indians riding inside the circle. Just before the dance ended, the Indians learned that some white men, who were frightened by the large gathering, were traveling to the valley to kill everyone. The Indians hid and the dance was never finished. The Ghost Dance soon disappeared from our area.

Grandma didn't know when our ancestors moved away from Cha:tiniu. A government surveyor, J. M. Anderson, identified an "Indian camp" at that locale on his 1882 and 1883 maps. His survey notes also confirm the presence of permanent settlers. There was a log fence around "Logan's ranch," where Logan lived in a log house. Near the meadow there was "the village of Chiquita containing 2 stores and 3 dwellings. . . . Harris & Wolff" ran one store and "Logan" the other. Log and split rail fences divided the land. Nearby was the trail to Jackass Meadow and "Basan's" Meadow, actually Beasore Meadow. Anderson also described white men he saw leading pack animals on the trail to Kaiser Creek.[4]

Other government surveys of the Sierra Nevada praised not only the land but also the timber. Yellow and sugar pines, fir, oak, and cedar were abundant.

If the family was still at Cha:tiniu in the early 1880s, the only reason for them to leave their ancestral home would have been the increasing number of settlers competing for the forest. For at Cha:tiniu everything was available to them; life was complete. When they finally did leave, it was westward, following the curve of the San Joaquin River, always settling nearby, on its west bank and where springs flowed freely.

Grandma said that for a short while in the mid-1880s, her parents lived at Soyakinu, a name that derives from *soyakanim,* meaning "ants' place." Some of our extended family already lived there, including the Jacksons, Norrises, Martins, and Burkheads. The white settler Joseph Kinsman also lived there with his Nɨm wife, Mary, and their children on land that he'd homesteaded. Mary was also one of my family's relatives. This area is now called Kinsman Flat.

History marks the family's next several moves. My great-grandparents, Jim and Lizzie Moore, lived at Tɨnobi for a while, near Kana'au, known today as Lion Point. On a brisk fall day in 1992 we visited Kana'au. We traveled a dirt road that exited Mammoth Pool Road, driving around trees whose low-hanging boughs brushed the top of the vehicle, until we were stopped by thick underbrush. We walked on. I carried our then infant grandson, Anthony, while Judy and our daughter, Jacquie, chattered their way behind. Kana'au was quiet in late afternoon. I was very aware of my ancestors who lived here about one hundred years ago; aware of my grandparents playing children's games while my great-grandmother cared for the family and my great-grandfather hunted the abundant wild game.

Grandma said that she was born at Kana'au in a cedar bark house. She thought it might have been in the mid-1880s, a year determined by Presbyterian mission officials near North Fork when Grandma required an official birthdate after she was taken there.

Soon after Grandma's birth, her dad built a small cabin of wood boards. It's long gone now, but we found the cabin's stone chimney, the sole reminder of the family's life there.

My great-grandparents' next move downriver was a direct result of the federal government's actions in the early 1890s. Western cattlemen, intent on preserving the mountain meadows for cattle grazing, and eastern conservationists, intent on managing the forests, successfully lobbied legislation through Congress that established the Sierra Timber Reserve in February 1893. Initially the reserve included more than four million forested acres, including much of the Nɨm's traditional territory. Management of the reserve ensured long-term use by several vested interests: timber, water, grazing, and mining. Local ranchers sat on the original grazing review boards that determined who was eligible to graze livestock. Inasmuch as U.S. citizenship and ownership of private land were conditions for issuance of a grazing permit, the Nɨm were left out; for it wasn't until 1924 that American Indians became citizens in their own country.

Grandpa couldn't remember the year, but he insisted there was a time when "forest men rounded up all of the cattle the Indians had in the forests and took them away, and no one was ever paid."

The Sierra Timber Reserve became the Sierra National Forest in 1897, during President William McKinley's administration. But its boundaries were not finally established until 1908, after President Theodore Roosevelt transferred considerable acreage to other national forests.

One of Grandpa's childhood memories was seeing suntati, meaning "uniformed soldiers," who, he said, were tuma'asi, meaning "men with black skins." "They were riding horses in the forest." That's all he knew about them.

The tuma'asi were "colored troopers" from the U.S. Army's 24th Infantry, 9th Cavalry, who were stationed at Yosemite National Park from 1899 to 1903. They were but one troop of many acting as an expeditionary force from 1891 until 1909, with orders to rid the park of herds of sheep that were supposedly damaging the federally protected forests and grasses. The soldiers Grandpa saw were outside the park's boundaries; occasionally they did leave the park to scour the Sierra National Forest.

On June 27, 1896, a man identified as Mr. Camino (the family name of Grandpa Willie's mother, Kitty) was found grazing sheep near Jackass Meadow. Two months later, on August 15, Troop K, 4th Cavalry, from Camp Wawona, marched eleven miles to Red's Meadow, scouting toward the southeast corner of Yosemite Park. They took two Winchester rifles from Indians named Charley and Cususe. Cususe could have been the late Housen Lavell, who lived in that area. His Nɨm name was Kasus. On June 17, 1897, another expedition left Camp Wawona to round up sheep at Beasore and Jackass meadows.

Regulatory procedures developed in 1897 effectively closed the Sierra National Forest to habitation, although it was several years until all of the Nɨm families living within its boundaries moved away. My great-grandparents left Tɨnobi shortly after 1900, Grandma said. By then it was increasingly difficult for her dad to find a place for his family to live.

Between 1848 and 1880 California's Indians not only lost their "right" to continue living on ancestral, or any other, land, a right guaranteed to them by the Treaty of Guadalupe Hidalgo, but they were also denied the legal means to acquire title. At least until the 1850s federal policy generally supported the right of Indian tribes to maintain communal landholdings and their traditional social and political activities. Problems surfaced when a few politicians, social reformers, and private financial interests, whose motivations varied from a sincere wish to benefit Indians to a thinly veiled desire to obtain the land on which they lived, recommended that land lived on traditionally by individual tribes be parceled to Indian families "to promote assimilation."

As the westward advance continued the federal commissioner of Indian affairs began persuading many tribes outside California to agree to allot tribal land to individual families, to be held solely by them. This policy was abolished in 1887 when Congress passed the General Allotment Act, usually referred to as the Dawes Act. This legislation eliminated the need to gain tribal consent to allotment designations and permitted any qualified Indian to settle on unappropriated public domain. He could then obtain forty acres that could be irrigated, or eighty acres of farmland that could not be irrigated, or one hundred sixty acres of grazing land.

In California the Dawes Act (which established the legal framework for current allotment law) enabled some mountain-dwelling Indians to gain title to land administered by the government in the federal forests. But a companion, and equally damaging, policy determined that after all eligible Indians received an allotment, the remaining former tribal lands were considered surplus federal land. Settlers, farmers, and ranchers were then permitted to either buy or homestead what was once Indian land, resulting in the Indians' loss of two-thirds of the state's total acreage, including Nim territory.

Most of California's Indians were under constant pressure to move from one place to another, and were unaware they could no longer live wherever they chose. Prior to 1887, most Indian families were not allowed to acquire land under the general homestead act. By the time the Dawes Act was passed in 1887, in our territory much of the mountain land had already been claimed by settlers. The only Indian families who benefited from the homestead act or who could purchase property were those in which a marriage existed between an Indian woman and a white man; he negotiated the legal process.

Perhaps pressured by forest rangers or by settlers, after Great-grandpa Jim left Kana'au he moved the family only short distances several times within a very few years. The San Joaquin River was also nearby, to the east. They lived at Sagwanoi, the name for the caterpillar worm that lives on the wildflowers called Farewell to Spring, a popular fishing camp in the old days near today's Redinger Lake. Within a year or two, they moved to Musa, also near today's Redinger Lake. This was Nooni's home; she was an old lady who was my great-grandfather's relative. In another year or so, he moved the family again, back upriver a short distance to Peyakgatɨ, which means "a thicket of grapevines." There he built two huts by a spring above the river.

They moved once again, finally settling at Peyakinu, meaning "place of grapes," south of today's Italian Bar Road and several miles west of the river. Grandpa John's childhood memories of Peyakinu remained vivid, even in his ninetieth year. He said he was born there in a cedar bark house. His Dad acquired more hogs. "The old man [as he called his father] ran hundreds of hogs. They died. They were poisoned. Ate poisoned grain. It was an accident." The "old man" then built a one-room frame house for the growing family and planted lots of fruit trees. "My mother had a big garden: squash, and beans, and tomatoes. Lots of deer then, go outside and 'boom.' Plenty of salmon. No more now." The cabin's walls collapsed years ago.

When they were children Mom and Aunt Ethel spent a lot of time with their grandparents at Peyakinu. A favorite pastime, Mom said, was walking from the cabin over a winding trail to fish in the San Joaquin River. As we drove to Redinger Lake in the spring of 1993 Mom pointed to a break in the brush where a paved road now crosses over the old trail from Peyakinu to the river. A few months later, on a jaunt to gather basket material alongside one of the many creeks that empty into the river, we followed a portion of another trail Mom walked with her Grandma Lizzie, from Peyakinu down to the river.

Before those happy days, the Nɨm were slowly moving out of the forest and closer to North Fork. C. Hart Merriam, an ethnographer who visited the area in 1902, found quite a few Indian camps in and around North Fork, near Crane Valley, and at the San Joaquin River. Rev. W. B. Noble, a minister of the Presbyterian church, visited North Fork just a few months later.

We are here in the heart of the Mono country. These Indians are
scattered far and wide, up and down the foothills, . . . more nu-
merously on the higher slopes of the Sierras. . . . Their mountain
home, however, gives them a security from encroachments of the
white man. . . . For although there is no Indian Reservation, the
sanctity of the Forest Reserve affords them a permanent and secure
retreat.[5]

A sanctity that was short-lived.

Although the forests were legally closed to settlement, some Nɨm
families benefited from federal legislation passed on June 25, 1910.
The law awarded American Indians who applied for them allotments of federal forestlands of between 100 and 160 acres, if the
acreage was chiefly valuable for agriculture or grazing and if the
Indians lived or had improvements on the land on June 25, 1910.

Ray Boothe, a Sierra National Forest supervisor who assigned
allotments to heads of families, assumed the allotments were
awarded for land "that these Indians or their forefathers had been
living on for, in some cases, many generations."[6] These original
trust patents entitled an Indian or his immediate heirs to occupy
the land for twenty-five years, after which, if they still lived there,
they received a final patent. But then the property became fee land
to be taxed by the county. Boothe estimated "probably less than
5%" of the twenty-five or thirty allotments he handled in one year
were still occupied in 1940.

The lack of occupancy may not always have been by choice.
Great-grandpa Jim was awarded a 120-acre allotment at Peyakinu
on March 24, 1920. The acreage is now public land; the family
doesn't know what became of the allotment. But I believe that, like
so many other Nɨm, my great-grandfather was unaware that his
property reverted to fee land twenty-five years after he received the
allotment. Thus from 1945 on, as were so many other California
Indians, he was unaware that he needed to pay property taxes, and
he might have lost the land. Or he may have sold it to a white man

Unidentified members of Jim and Lizzie Moore's family heading for the vineyards at Mentone for the summer harvest in the mid-1920s. (Author's collection)

who was purchasing other Indian allotments as well as settlers' homesteads. Nevertheless, my great-grandfather was still living there when he died in 1948.

As the old way of life—hunting, gathering, fishing freely in the forests—was denied them, my ancestors as well as other Nɨm families occasionally worked for white people to support their families. Many of the Nɨm Noble met in the summer of 1902 harvested grapes at San Joaquin Valley vineyards, as they had since 1900. Mom remembers that childhood experience, too, when the family traveled to Mentone each summer to pick grapes.

CHAPTER NINE

WHEN THE DAYS TURN COOL

The energy identified today as nature speaks to us in many ways. The sun going back in the sky, the night air becoming more brisk, the days turning cool—all are variations directing our lives. My family calls this time *yɨbanotɨ,* "when the days turn cool."

Mountain residents enjoy the brilliant orange, yellow, and red leaves that hang from tree branches, awaiting a sudden dip in temperature to break loose and drop lazily onto the ground. They know it is fall.

Squirrels perch on tall branches, gossiping cheerfully as they pluck cones that grow on Ponderosa and bull pines. As they feast on the nuts, the burrs drop from their busy hands to litter the forest floor. Some cones evade the hungry squirrels, breaking free and falling onto the ground. Acorns join nature's harvest, dropping from oak trees, skipping along the ground to rest, hidden in piles of fallen leaves.

In the old days, as yɨbanotɨ came around, my ancestors began to gather their belongings and return to their winter homes. Refreshed after a few days rest, they refurbished the tonobi, their cedar bark houses, either adding fresh bark to existing tonobi or rebuilding them. The tonobi was comfortable for its purpose, just large enough for the family to sleep in or to seek shelter during winter's inclement weather. Most of the family's time was otherwise spent outdoors, pursuing each day's activities.

Wa´ap, cedar bark, was the preferred building material because of its virtual imperviousness to insect damage. It is also fire resistant, and because it retains heat, a tonobi warmed with a small fire inside remained comfortable no matter the outside temperature. Smoke escaped from an opening at the top. The doorway was covered with tanned deerskin.

Cedar bark was usually gathered about a year after the tree fell from old age; the trees were never cut prematurely. Grandma said a tonobi stood about twelve feet tall and was conical in shape. The bark boards were stacked vertically, notched at the top so they fit snugly together without the need of additional support. But Mom recalled seeing tonobi in her childhood that were built with the boards supported inside by four sturdy poles from live oaks.

Most people made a ditch in the ground around the outside of the tonobi to deter water from entering, but even with space between the boards rain didn't enter. Some people also made a "raincoat" of bunchgrass tied with grapevines that was placed over the top half of the tonobi. I've built three tonobi on our property; after heavy rain the ground inside isn't wet, even though the ground outside is saturated. Grandma said that after the white man arrived, sometimes entrances were constructed in a shape similar to that of the Eskimo's igloo, requiring people to crouch to enter. Perhaps this was a way of discouraging strangers from entering the home without invitation.

When the settlement was in shape the men resumed fishing and hunting while the women enjoyed the season's gleanings.

After the dry season of tazewano, the first rain softened the ground, awakening kɨa´, the female of the rain beetle species. Kɨa´ is dug from her two-foot-deep underground home by widening her hole, which is easy to find as it's about as big around as one's

Left to right: Kitty Camino Pomona, the author's great-grandmother; Mary Paiute; Annie Bethel; Emma McSwain; and Maggie Jim, on October 5, 1902. They are sitting in front of one of the women's cedar bark houses, a few miles northwest of North Fork, near today's Road 274. All of the baskets pictured were used regularly. (Photograph by C. Hart Merriam. Courtesy of The Bancroft Library.)

index finger. After collecting a bucketful, the kɨa´ are thrown onto hot coals and cooked until they pop. The abdomen is delicious, tasting like well-cooked meat fat, but without the fat. Our family still looks for kɨa´.

In the old days women used a poto, our indigenous shovel, to dig up the kɨa´. After a straight mountain mahogany branch of varying length and dimension was selected, the leaves and then the bark were peeled off. One end was fashioned into a point with a knife made of obsidian and hardened in a fire. Grandma always carried her poto when she walked, especially through tall grass, swinging it back and forth as she sang a song to Rattlesnake, alerting him of her approach. If frisky children didn't obey, her poto was swatted across legs, quickly commanding attention. Just ask me! And it was a fine cane, too. Our family still makes poto for a variety of tasks.

The bulb, or root, of the soap plant was dug up with a poto. This plant is deciduous and reappears each spring; it has long tapered leaves and flowers during tazewano, on a very tall stalk. Flakes from the bulb were used for soap, and part of the bulb was fashioned into a brush. Mom and Aunt Ethel, who learned how to make brushes from their Grandma Lizzie, still make them occasionally.

It's not the making of the brush that's difficult, it's digging it up in early fall from hard-baked ground, but that's when the bulb is best for making soaproot brushes. Instead of using a poto, Mom and Auntie now use steel shovels, digging to a depth of about a foot. Sometimes they "fudge," digging the bulbs in late spring when the soil is still soft; but that early the bulb's skin hasn't broken down to fiber quite as thickly as is preferred. It's the fiber that is the foundation of the brush; where it wraps around the bulb's base, the fiber forms a natural bend or hook, ideal for brushing. If the bulb is large, only one is needed for each brush, but sometimes more than one is used. Some bulbs are lighter in color than others. I've watched Mom use fiber off three bulbs, the center almost blond and the outsides darker. Its quite artistic, which is her intent.

The fiber is carefully removed from the bulb, and the dirt is cleaned off with an always handy twig. The narrow end is tied with string, which was made from milkweed in the old days, gathered when the plant's stalk had dried and was easily pried apart. The brittle stalk was rolled back and forth on the thigh until it bound together as an exceptionally strong string. Mom and Auntie now use store-bought string.

The bulb is roasted in the hot coals of a fire for a couple of hours, until it softens into a sticky mucilage. We experimented a few years ago, cooking two bulbs in a microwave oven at a high setting for twenty minutes. They were soft enough to use, but with a texture that Mom and Auntie didn't like. So much for modern, time-saving inventions. The mucilage is scraped off of the bulb with a stick and applied several times to the tied end of the brush, each application hardening during a process that takes two to three days. The brush now has a solid handle.

Soap brushes are great, so long as they remain dry; when wet, the handle softens and loses its shape. They last for years. We take one with us when gathering mushrooms, to brush off the soil, and we also use it to clean furniture and car upholstery. Soap brushes can also be used as brooms; a long, straight branch is tied to the end of the fibers before the glue is applied.

Mom and Auntie still use soap brushes to sweep scattered acorn flour back into a pounding hole. They were also used as hairbrushes and to clean animal skins, but they are seldom used that way now.

While visiting encampments near North Fork during the fall of 1902, Merriam saw "lots of acorn mush. They [the families] had 4 or 5 children (all young) and lots of dogs and cats." At another encampment, "quantities of shucked acorns were drying and fresh acorn mush was plenty in the cooking baskets. At the lower camp was a pile of just roasted cones of Digger pines with a pile of thick scales just hammered off with a stone, and a *chem-ey'-ah* [sic] basket ½ full of the roasted nuts."[1]

Acorn, as we describe the cooked product, was eaten in the old days with every meal, usually accompanying meat or fish. The actual gathering of these very important nuts began when they started falling from the trees. If the weather was exceptionally mild and the family remained longer at the higher elevations, they began gathering acorns there, storing the nuts in granaries, to be carried later in the women's large conical baskets back to their winter homes.

The women of those families who still cook acorn have special places to which they return year after year. Mutual respect prevails,

so that families avoid each other's gathering places. It's more difficult to gather now, though. Fences prevent access to traditional
places throughout Nɨm territory. Fortunately, white friends alert
Mom and Auntie that acorns are dropping off of oak trees on their
property, and off they go.

Several varieties of oak trees grow in Nɨm territory, but the most
favored for making acorn is the nut of *wiyap,* the black oak, because
it cooks up to a thick, evenly consistent finished product. Wiyap
produces a somewhat greasy nut, so acorns from *yaga,* the white
oak, are also processed and mixed with wiyap when the acorns are
pounded. Mom is one of several ladies, including Aunt Ethel, who
still cook acorn, although the process is less tedious than in the old
days, when Mom learned from and helped her Grandma Lizzie.

Acorns are always gathered after they fall from the tree. In the old
days, however, if there were still acorns in storage from the previous year, sometimes green acorns were knocked out of trees and
mixed with the previous year's crop for better flavor. The family
used a pole, made from a fifteen to twenty-foot-long willow or bull
pine branch that was stripped of its twigs and bark, to knock them
down.

Mom spends many days gathering acorns before she even begins
to process them. Much of her effort now was once shared by entire
families to provide sufficient acorn to feed everyone throughout the
year. Basket loads were carried on the women's backs during the
seasonal gathering. Mom carries her acorns in a large gunnysack.

In the old days several conical-shaped granaries were built to
store acorns. Moistureproof bunchgrass was laid thickly, and without openings, over a framework made with buttonbush sticks that
were set on a several-foot-high platform of live oak branches.
Straps made from the flannel bush tied the granary together. This
innovative storage protected the nuts from hungry animals, especially from the prying hands of squirrels who don't know how to
spread apart the protecting grass. Mom says that when snowfall
was much heavier years ago, her Grandma Lizzie made the plat-

forms so high she had to climb a ladder made of live oak branches so she could reach the granary. Mom stores acorns in boxes on the front porch, but a few years ago she built an innovative granary shaped like a rectangular box, made with chicken wire and supported by four wooden legs; the box is covered with a tarp. She keeps tradition, though, by putting two buckeye nuts inside to protect the acorns from getting worms. Her modern granary works just fine.

White people think acorn preparation is a time-consuming, tedious task. But that's what women did in those days, Mom says. "They didn't have any clocks. Just got up in the morning and went to bed at night and knew what they had to do in between."

Mom usually processes acorn out-of-doors. She first cracks each shell with a small rock she keeps for that purpose and leaves the acorns to dry for a few days to more easily remove the nut from the shell. After the shell is taken off the nut and it dries for a couple more days, its red skin is easily scraped off. Mom then flips and shakes the nuts in her winnowing basket, so that any foreign material is blown away.

Modern corn grinders or food processors now enable women to grind the acorn into *ebina,* what we call the flour, but Mom still occasionally uses a *paha,* a stone tool usually called a pestle by non-Indians, to pound her nuts in a *tacoiya,* a shallow hole formed in bedrock granite or in a portable granite rock. Non-Indians call these holes mortars. She uses her soap brush to periodically sweep the ebina out of the hole into a basket, or brushes it back into the hole from the sides of the mortar if it requires more pounding. Mom remembers watching her Grandma Lizzie build a tall three-sided or curved structure of chaparral branches around the pounding rock to stop the wind from scattering the ebina as she pounded her acorn.

The deeper holes in bedrock granite weren't used to pound acorns, Mom said, because it's too hard to remove ebina from them. Instead these holes were used to coarsely pound a variety of seeds.

Margaret Moore Bobb *(right)* and her first cousin, Annie Jackson Lewis *(left),* in the 1940s, pounding acorn into flour behind Mrs. Bobb's home at Tɨpoki. (Author's collection)

Ebina must be leached with water to remove its bitter tannic acid. When my ancestors lived near running streams, they laid ebina in a shallow basin in the sand and diverted the stream in a gentle flow over the basin. A branch from a white fir or cedar was placed on the sand just above the ebina to slow the water's flow. The tannic acid was leached out after several hours, and the ebina was then lifted from the sand with the heel of the hand, without lifting any sand, a method Mom insists was foolproof because "we knew what we were doing."

After the Nɨm were forced to live away from free-flowing streams, an innovative leaching basin was created. Women built a waist-high frame with live oak limbs, layering the top with slender sticks a couple of inches deep and putting sand on top of the sticks. Then the ebina was put on the sand, and water, which was

Margaret Moore Bobb leaching acorn flour at a spring behind her home at Tɨpoki in the late 1950s. (Author's collection)

hauled from nearby springs for daily use, was poured slowly over it until it was leached.

Grandma didn't have a water well until the mid-1970s. I'd haul buckets and buckets of water from a nearby spring so she could leach her ebina on her platform structure, built under the shade of an old tree behind our house. To save time she laid the ebina on muslin instead of sand. After her well was drilled, Grandma was able to run a slow stream of hose water over her ebina, and I was able to play more.

Kawan is what we call the leached but not yet cooked acorn. It's moist from the leaching and tastes very sweet, quickly attracting impish fingers to slyly, or so Gloria and I thought, scoop some into our mouths. "Don't eat the kawan," Grandma and Mom often admonished us, "or your hair will turn white." Neither of us paid attention, and guess what? We both grayed prematurely.

In the old days kawan was squeezed once through the fingers onto mats and air-dried. It was then stored in baskets, sometimes for up to a year, but it had to be checked occasionally because a weevil, similar to the rice weevil, could invade it. Now Mom and Aunt Ethel usually store kawan in their freezers.

Mom begins cooking kawan early in the morning, first heating several cylindrical soapstone rocks—she calls them her "cooking rocks"—in a hot fire. Grandma gathered these rocks years ago from a creek bed alongside Highway 168, about halfway between Prather and the San Joaquin Valley. Mom takes good care of them because that land is now privately owned and we've been told to keep away.

While the rocks are heating Mom mixes the kawan with water in a large bucket. On special occasions she still uses a cooking basket. Additional pails of water wait nearby (baskets held the extra water in the old days). Her cooking utensils are traditional. Two long poles, made with mountain mahogany branches that are stripped of their bark, are used to lift the stones from the fire. A bull pine branch, forced into the oval shape of a spoon and tied with purchased string (milkweed string was used in the old days), is used to stir the rocks. Some women sometimes used the harder-to-manipulate oak wood for stirring spoons.

When the rocks become so hot they are white, Mom deftly lifts them out of the fire with her poles onto a flat rock, where she pours water over them to wash off the ash. She then lifts the rocks into the cooking bucket, immediately stirring them with her spoon, lifting and moving them through the bubbling mixture, occasionally adding more water. As the rocks cool they are removed to the fire and replaced with hot ones.

Skill is required for every procedure. If one of Mom's grandsons is around, he helps out by handling the rocks that must be lifted correctly or they'll fall to the ground, and you get yelled at. Just ask me! An exact amount of water must be used to properly thicken kawan. If Mom is asked, "How much water?" she replies, "Just

Margaret Moore Bobb cooking acorn in a twined basket behind her home at Tɨpoki in the late 1950s. By stirring the mixture with her specially made stick, she prevents it from burning or sticking to the basket. The two coiled baskets in the photograph were used to store the acorn. (Author's collection)

enough." The boiling kawan must be stirred at a specific speed to prevent the rocks from burning both the emulsion and the basket. She decides the kawan is cooked by either observing its texture as it drips from her stirring spoon or using the age-old cook's taste test, dipping her finger into it. When she smiles, it's done. The kawan is then poured into large containers (a coiled basket woven especially for storing acorn was used not so long ago), if it's not eaten up before then. Smooth and delicious, that's the mark of a good cook, such as Mom and Auntie.

The cooked kawan has several consistencies. We call it *yumana* when it's stirred until it's a thick emulsion, similar to a milk shake. If it's cooked longer, until it's similar to Jell-O and retains its shape when scooped out, we call it *ekibe*. *Konowoi* is cooked like ekibe, but a dipperful is dropped into cold water, causing it to form an oval shape that is then lifted out. Also, small amounts of kawan can be put on a flat rock that is kept hot by placing it next to the fire pit; after it's fried, it looks like a Mexican tortilla. We call this *kumasa,* which is now the generic word for all types of bread.

To hasten the cooking process now, the few women who still process acorn sometimes cook kawan in a metal pot on the stove. Mom usually still cooks it out-of-doors, putting her pot on a grate over the same open fire in which she heats the rocks. She still cooks with rocks, even in a metal pot, because they add a distinct flavor and maintain a semblance of an age-old tradition. Mom also sometimes uses a shovel instead of the poles, long metal spoons instead of the bull pine stirring spoons, and jars and pans for storage instead of baskets.

Acorns were a prized trade commodity in the old days. During one of his forays into the Sierra Nevada in the 1860s, John Muir met several Indians he identified as Monos, walking from east of the Sierra Nevada "on their way to Yosemite for a load of acorns." He was horrified by their appearance: the "dirt on some of their faces seemed almost old enough and thick enough to have a geological significance." Muir's observation is actually quite funny. I can imagine him suffering from many mosquito bites while the "queer, hairy, muffled creatures" protected themselves by covering their exposed skin with dirt.[2] Grandpa said that covering the body with dirt not only prevents annoying mosquito bites but also protects against sunburn.

Occasionally Mom trades or sells either unleached or leached flour, or cooked acorn, to other Indians. That, too, is traditional.

In the old days when daytime temperatures began to dip and nights were brisk, about when the family was gathering acorns, each year a messenger came from east of the Sierras announcing it was time to meet with some of my ancestors and others, sibiti Nɨm friends (identified today by many people as Mono Lake Paiutes), near the divide of the Sierra Nevada. There they traded for the delicious nuts produced by the thickly needled piñon trees that grow in the mountains, foothills, and high desert to the east.

Sometimes my ancestors did cross the Sierra to gather piñon. But because the sibiti Nɨm also enjoyed eating acorn, and oak trees are not indigenous to their territory, sometimes they traveled to meet the Nɨm at various places in the high Sierras to trade piñons for acorns. Grandma remembered traveling to the sibiti Nɨm to trade; she said it was a good time, visiting, feasting, and playing games. Whole families made the trek, walking or riding horseback for several days on any of the trails that cross the Sierras and camping along the way. Grandma said each woman carried a *wono* on her back, the large conical-shaped basket used for hauling loads, filled with acorns or salt grass to trade for the piñons they would carry home.

"I can remember seeing them coming for miles—the trails those days were just wide enough for a horse—in the lead was always the old buck Indian on a pony and sometimes two or three years old tot was riding with him," recalled Dulce Tully Rose.

> There would be the pack horse or horses with a number of supplies and then the Indian ladies with the kids trailing. All walked—they always walked and the squaws would sometimes have babies strapped to their heads. We'd see them coming and get off to the side of the trail and let them have the trail. A lot of the kids I went to school with. They would come back in the Fall and go to school in North Fork. They were packing piñon nuts from the other side.[3]

Grandpa John remembered, when he was a boy, walking "the trail past a lake toward postpile [now the Devils Postpile National Monument]. They [the vertical stone slabs] used to be lumber, now rock, to trade dry kawan for sacks of piñon, big and orange. They [the piñons] lay on sand waiting to be picked."

When I was a child each fall we drove across the Sierras to Mono

Lake or Bishop to either trade for piñons or gather our own. Mom drove us through Yosemite National Park and down the Sierra's eastern slope on the then-tortuous single-lane Tioga Road that wound down the mountainside. In the distance was Mono Lake. This is how an island in the lake was created.

Deer and Bear were sisters-in-law. Both had two children apiece. Mother Bear was angry at her sister-in-law and wanted to kill her. So Bear thought up an idea to kill Mother Deer. When morning came Deer and Bear went in search of food. While searching for their meal, Deer was scratching her head. Bear kept watching Deer scratch. This kept up for quite a long time. Bear called to her, "Sister-in-law, come here and I will see what you have on your head." Deer came over and Bear looked in Deer's hair. She found lice in her hair. Bear said to Deer, "Oh, my, you have lice." All this time Bear pretended deer had lice. Bear said, "I will pick them out for you." So she pretended to look for lice. She then lifted her big paw and hit Deer on the back of the neck. Deer fell to the ground, dead. Bear panicked and realized she had done something terrible. She told herself, "Now I have to take care of the two fawns and my own two cubs." Bear returned to her cedar bark house. The four children were playing out front. She decided to tell the two little fawns that their mother had an accident and was killed. When she told the little fawns, they started crying. They sang a song, saying, "Pu pu snab a puick, pu pu snab a puick, pu pu snab a puick." The next morning Mother Bear called her two cubs outside. She told them to try and smother the two fawns in the cedar bark house. Then she left her two cubs and went searching for food. The cubs and the fawns were playing outside. Inside the cedar bark house a small fire was burning. The four little ones decided to play hide-and-seek. The two little fawns said they would hide inside the cedar bark house. One of the cubs shut the door behind them. The smoke filled the cedar bark house quite rapidly. The fawns started to gasp for air. Somehow they found holes in the cedar bark house. Our houses were made of cedar bark so this left cracks in the walls. The fawns stuck their noses through the cracks. They stayed in there for a long while. The little cubs opened the door and out ran the fawns. The fawns had white noses and smoke-grayed hair. To this day they are this color. They started laughing and laughing, saying that was fun and the two little cubs should try it. The two little cubs went inside the cedar bark house. They started choking and coughing. They were smothered in an instant. The fawns opened the door and waited for the two little cubs, but they didn't appear. The fawns walked in and found them dead on the floor. They got scared and said, "What do we do? Our aunt will come back and kill us." They dragged the two cubs outside and placed them on the swings. The two fawns decided to run away before Mother Bear came home. Mother Bear came back that evening. Before she reached the cedar bark house she wondered if her cubs had done what she told them about, smothering the fawns. She reached the yard and looked around. Her two cubs were playing on the swings. She didn't see the two little fawns anywhere. She walked over to the swings and asked if the little fawns were around, but she didn't get any answer. She touched one of her little cubs and he fell over. She saw that the little fawns had killed her two little cubs. She said she would revenge the death of her two cubs. She looked around and found the tracks of the two little fawns. She followed the fawns' tracks to the home of Tiger. [There really is a tiger living in the mountains, insisted Grandma, not a mountain lion but "striped, like in the circus."] Tiger lived near Rock Creek. Tiger told the two little fawns to hide in her basket. When Bear got there and asked Tiger if she had seen the fawns, Tiger said, "No." Bear looked around and left. Tiger told the two fawns Bear had left. So they went on their way. Mother Bear was a little way behind them. After the fawns left Tiger discovered their hoofprints on her basket. We use this design on baskets now. They went to Yauyautɨ [at Chiquito Ridge, northeast of Mammoth Pool] and spent the night there. The two fawns reached Mono Lake on the third day. There they met Piweshamuda, the

giant, and asked him to stretch his legs across the lake for them to
cross. They told him that Bear was after them because they killed
her two cubs and that Bear had killed their mother. Piweshamuda,
the giant, stretched his legs across the lake and they ran across. Bear
reached Mono Lake where Piwashemuda lived. She asked him if he
would stretch his legs for her to cross. She said that she wanted to
catch the fawns to take them home and care for them since their
mother had been killed. Bear started across and got halfway across
when Piweshamuda pulled his legs back. Bear fell into the water
and drowned. There is a black island in the center of Mono Lake.
That is Bear. The lake has a little worm which the Indians in the east
call *kwɨzub*.   —as told by Grandma

Negit Island in Mono Lake is really the bear, Grandma said.

After we reached Mono Lake I'd search the sky for flocks of birds
we call nutcrackers; he enjoys eating piñons as much as we do.
Nutcrackers circle above ripe cones that have fallen to the ground,
leading people to gathering areas. We'd find fallen cones that had
already opened; it was easy to pry the nuts loose. Sometimes we'd
arrive before the nutcrackers, so we had to gather the unripened
cones, but by warming the cones next to a fire the piñon nuts pop
right out. They can be eaten raw, but my family likes them best after
they're parched on a *yata,* a specially woven parching tray, by toss-
ing the nuts and hot coals together. Then the shells are easily
cracked and the nuts are eaten.

There were other journeys. Grandma enjoyed visiting her old
friend Minnie Mike, who lived on a knoll west of Mono Lake, to
trade her acorn flour for kwɨzub, the "little worm" from her story,
which was actually the larva or pupa that evolves into a brine fly
that lives in the lake's saline water. Sometimes Grandma joined
Minnie Mike and other Indian women who lived there, wading
fully clothed into the water among the calcium-deposited tufa
towers that mark the shoreline. They carried flat baskets to scoop
up the kwɨzub, returning to shore to lay the kwɨzub on the

The large island in Mono Lake is the Bear who was chasing the fawns across the Sierras. It is now called Negit Island. (Author's collection)

ground to dry in the warm sun. Grandma said that sometimes the women built bark platforms for the drying process. They rubbed the dried kwɨzub in their hands to loosen the thin, outer membrane and tossed them in a *chamaiya,* a winnowing basket, so that the wind blew away the membrane. Then kwɨzub was ready to eat or to store for later use.

Just thinking about it, I can smell kwɨzub. Grandma cooked them in boiling water; then she and Grandpa ate them with acorn. They thought kwɨzub was delicious, but I didn't like the fishy taste.

During a recent trip to Mono Lake I walked over the sticky mud on boards, in and around the tufa towers, to the water, where I scooped up handfuls of brine flies. Memories surfaced, rendered more poignant with the knowledge that only one family over there still gathers kwɨzub.

Forest fires, usually caused by lightning, were common in the old days, when they were allowed to burn as a natural way to clear underbrush. Fires weren't feared as destructive events because my ancestors understood their cleansing nature. They knew that fire created a long-term benefit to all life by annually eliminating underbrush and dry tinder.

When a fire approached their home it was easy for them to pack baskets with food and implements, gather together, and leave. If their homes burned they were rebuilt. Everything could be replaced.

Fire also created new and stronger growth on plants used for basket material. Mom said our family didn't intentionally burn brush to improve plants, but they knew that where fire occurred the new plants were improved. (Fire ash is a natural source of potassium important for the growth of healthy plants.)

After several winter seasons of little rain and mild winters, in 1990, Mom noticed the diminishing quality of basket material. The next year, when she went to Long Ridge, above the San Joaquin River, to gather sourberry "sticks" from a patch that had burned during a forest fire several months earlier, the young shoots were the favored straight and supple "sticks" she needed. Enough was gathered to get her through that year, and then some.

Grandpa said that if there were no forest fires in the old days, the Nɨm would intentionally burn the brush in the fall after it rained. "The Indians kept the brush and undergrowth burned off and there was no trouble in riding anywhere over the country in those days," Joseph Kinsman recalled in 1914. "The grass grew very high and there were all kinds of wild game. It was not uncommon to see a herd of 80 or 100 deer feeding or running across the country."[4]

After Sierra National Forest officials began to contain naturally caused forest fires, some families continued to intentionally light fires in the fall to burn the underbrush. Its practice depended on the current forest supervisor's personal philosophy. "Our first forest supervisor [Charles Shinn] was a brilliant [sic] and literary man," recalled Ranger Gene Tully, "but absolutely impractical as to field management." He described "the method employed by the

Indians and pioneer settlers who loved the forests and were as much interested in their protection as if they owned them legally. They employed the creeping fire method, scientifically used in no other than primative [sic] measures to prevent conflagration that would defy a thousand men to extinguish until it was ready to let them." But, added Tully, "our supervisor was emphatically opposed to the use of fire under any circumstances."[5]

"The Indian burns were practically gone before my time," reminisced Dulce Tully Rose. "I can remember them fussing about it in the Forest Service. . . . I don't remember seeing the Indians burn the forest. It could have happened but being a kid I never thought about it. . . . [T]his is what the Indians did. The forest was clean. There was no debris because they would start the fire low and by the time it burned up winter had set in and it couldn't go any further. The snow would put it out." Mrs. Rose assumed the fires were "for preservation of the game. So they would have grass for the next year."[6]

Here, where I still live at Tɨpoki, years ago each fall the Moore family took care of the forest with the slow-burn method. When I was a kid Grandpa let me help him burn the hillside behind our house to clean out the underbrush and to protect us from wildfires. After the first rainfall, he'd light the grass at the lowest elevation of our property; we'd wait nearby with wet sacks, to control the fire's direction as it crept slowly up the hillside, clearing the previous year's growth. In the 1960s a Forest Service supervisor told Grandpa to stop the burning. Now the hillsides surrounding us are covered with underbrush.

CHAPTER TEN

THE CHURCH, THE FOREST SERVICE, AND CHANGE

"The Indians are all going down to the North Fork to see the Priest," observed Joseph Kinsman.[1] By the end of the decade, according to Mrs. George Teaford, "white settlers [had] chased off the priest who was charging a dollar a piece for services."[2]

Catholic missionaries were probably the first religionists to visit the Nɨm. Their efforts at conversion were minimal, as most families continued their traditions and ceremonies. For eons past the grandparents in my extended family taught their grandchildren, imparting a way of life through example and stories. But when in the early 1900s the federal government and the Christian church combined forces to forcibly remove Nɨm children from their homes to attend a missionary boarding school, this unique method of teaching was sorely tested. Cultural genocide was the long-term result.

After he visited North Fork in 1903, Dr. Noble observed,

And now I want to tell you of another field for Indian work. I found the region about North Fork swarming with Indians and half breeds. . . . Mr. Shinn, the Head Ranger, a very intelligent man and a Christian (Congregationalist) is anxious to have something done

for the Indians. Mr. Frederic, a Presbyterian, a school teacher of
many years experience in the region, also told me much of the condition and needs of these Indians. There is no reservation, some
own their land, others are but squatters, but as the land on which
they live is of little value they are unmolested by the whites. Their
rancherias [settlements] are scattered about everywhere. They live
by the men working in the logging camps and in herding cattle and
sheep, and the women washing gold in the creeks, and (in season)
picking grapes in the San Joaquin Valley. They are more numerous
than the white population of the region. In the school where Mr.
Frederic has taught for years Indian pupils were in the majority. Yet
Mr. Shinn estimates that in general not more than one in twenty of
the Indian children goes to school at all. Morally their condition is
very deplorable. There is no government agent to prevent the sale of
liquor to the Indians. . . . [D]runkeness [sic] prevails. Their young
girls grow up only to be the victims of the licentiousness of white
men who actually buy them from their parents for ten or twenty dol-
lars a head! A large population of the children are half breeds. . . .
No religious work has ever been done among them so far as I have
learned except that a Catholic priest is said to have come among
them some years ago and labored for a short time, marrying some
who were living together in sin, baptizing children, but whom the
'squaw men' threatened to shoot if he did not leave.[3]

Dr. Noble scoffed at the Nim lifestyle; he was disturbed to find
some people continuing to live in "brush houses [and] compelled
to live on acorns and fish as their chief food supply."[4]

Mom believes the occasional sale of children to "squaw men"
was an adaptation of the dowry system, enabling those families
who did so to survive in the most dire circumstances. The dowry
system ended in the 1920s, as the missionaries exerted pressure to
stop the custom. As for alcohol, in the early days it was often offered in trade by whites to Indians, who initially had no idea of its
effect.

Dr. Noble, who envisioned a school for women run by women, appealed to a Miss Fraser:

> Now here is a problem for our Christianity to solve. It is a hard one, but I know the sad condition of these Indian women and girls will appeal to the sympathy of all the members of your society.
>
> [If there were a school] . . . in which some of the Indian girls might find a shelter during the period of their life in which they are in most danger and be trained to virtue, at least one element of the need would be met. But others might also be reached, and the work to be extended to both sexes. Mr. Shinn and Mr. Frederick would be very helpful allies should a work be undertaken.[5]

In the 1890s and in the first few years of the twentieth century, some Nɨm families sent their children to public school. It wasn't always successful. Mrs. George Teaford recalled a school about three miles from The Forks (near today's Bass Lake):

> The little half-breed children and Indian children trudged happily to school one morning. But these children weren't to see the benefits of education yet. They were not allowed to attend school. Bitterly disappointed they turned their backs on school forever. Much of the bitterness still exists in the people who were excluded.[6]

In 1903 the Presbyterian church purchased land for its mission from Fred Visher and Ben Norris where they ran a saloon. It was on the east side of the dirt road that went from North Fork to Cascadel, only a few miles east of North Fork and next to where we now live. The existing buildings were remodeled into a comfortable home for Nɨm girls, who were to be taught Christianity and trained to become better housewives.

Rev. Alexander Hood and his wife arrived at the North Fork mission in 1910 to administer a school of several teachers to guide the sixty grammar school-aged girls, who had been taken from their

The girls' dormitory at the North Fork Presbyterian Indian Mission east of Cascadel Road. The author's aunt, Ethel Pomona Temple, lost her "pretty pink dress" when the dormitory burned down in the early 1930s. (Author's collection)

homes throughout the area. Within a year, the complex included a church with a belfry and bell and a main building that contained the girls' dormitory, dining room, kitchen, and chapel. Other buildings quartered Mr. Hood's family and the faculty.

Grandma was among the first children to attend the mission school. She never forgot the day missionaries came to her parents' home at Peyakinu and took her away. Her parents could do nothing to prevent their firstborn child from leaving. Tears flowed, she said. Tuhiwi, as her parents named her, was renamed Margaret by one of the missionaries, who considered it improper for Indian children to use their given names.

Grandma described her loneliness at the mission school, the

Jim Moore and his wife, Lizzie Capp Moore, who is holding their son, George, traveling to North Fork from their home at Peyakinu by horse and wagon in the early 1900s. In the back seat is another of their children, who is unidentified. (Author's collection)

whippings she endured when she spoke her native language. Her misery finally impelled her to run away, but when she returned home her parents took her back to the mission, Grandma said, because they had decided it was probably best for her to learn the white man's way of life.

While she was at the Presbyterian Mission School, Grandma's parents missed her so much that almost every weekend they made the several-hour journey by horse and buggy to visit her and, when they were old enough to be taken there, her sisters, Emma and Daisy. Grandma said she always looked forward to summer so she could return home.

At first boys didn't live at the North Fork mission or attend its school. So Grandpa and Grandpa John went to Castle Peak, a public school located near what is now the intersection of Road 225 and Italian Bar Road. Unlike the public school near The Forks, this school permitted Indian children to attend. Grandpa never went beyond the second grade; he kept running away, Grandpa John said in jest. Grandpa John didn't stay very long either. "Too far walk there when rain and snow. I stop going."

Two other brothers, Chanapa and Paiyuchu, were taken from their parents by agents of the Bureau of Indian Affairs to attend Sherman Institute, the bureau's nonreservation Indian boarding school near Riverside, California. Soon after they arrived there, Paiyuchu was renamed George and Chanapa was renamed Robert. Seventeen-year-old Robert's sudden death on May 14, 1915, following an accident while he played shot put at the boarding school, shocked the family, who immediately went into mourning, Grandma said. George, too, was only a teenager when he died of an illness; once again, the family mourned.

When she was in her midteens, Grandma decided she wanted a change of scene and also traveled to Sherman Institute to continue her education, but she only remained there a couple of years. She left to work as a maid "near Cucamonga," she said, just as she had been taught at the North Fork mission.

School-aged children from throughout the western United States attended Sherman Institute. The government's reason for removing Indian children from their parents was due in part to the prejudice against Indian children attending public schools, which near North Fork at least was obviously not the case. In spite of all the concerns about racial prejudice in elementary school, Mom and Aunt Ethel, Grandma, Grandpa, and Grandpa John and his wife, Daisy, had no memory of prejudice during their childhood. "We just had fun and learned," Mom said.

When boys were eventually admitted to the North Fork mission school, they, too, were taught Christianity, and how to be farmers, fruit growers, cattlemen, and mechanics.

Elsewhere in California the church was joined by citizens who were genuinely concerned about the Indians' eroding conditions. When it became public knowledge in 1904 that the 1851 treaties were never ratified, these people demanded that the federal gov-

A teenaged Margaret
Moore about 1912.
(Author's collection)

ernment correct the situation. Realizing it could no longer ignore
the effect of its policies and actions, the government appointed
C. E. Kelsey as its special agent to conduct an intense study of the
problem.

As Kelsey traveled around the state he was dismayed by the effect the failed treaties had on the Indians, particularly in the northern part. He recommended that the 1887 Indian Allotment Act be
applied to any Indians who lacked fee title to any land. Kelsey was
an astute observer. He was particularly concerned about the lack

of education for Indian children: "[In the] matter of schooling for their children all Indian children were refused admission to public schools . . . and public sentiment is against their admission. About the only districts in which Indian children are welcome are those small ones which are likely to lapse if the Indians do not attend." Of the North Fork mission Kelsey observed,

> There are also quite a number of Indians located within the boundaries of the forest reserves. They have, of course, no title to the land they occupy, and since the establishment of the forest reserves, it is uncertain whether the lands within the boundaries can legally be allotted to them. These bands have mostly been in their present location from time immemorial, and there seems to be no occasion for any action in respect to any of them. The Forest Reserve officials do not seem to object to the Indians, though some of them desire to extend their hold by means of leases or permits which it is proposed to have the Indians secure to entitle them to reside upon the reserve.[7]

The government acted on Kelsey's report in 1906. It authorized land purchases for the state's homeless Indians, who were to be assigned to rancherias that the government planned to develop as Indian communities. The first land purchased in this general area was a half section in Hudson Basin (also known as Jose Basin), east of the San Joaquin River and northeast of Auberry. One hundred acres were surveyed into five-acre tracts for homesite allotments to the Nɨm and unapatɨ Nɨm living in the area.

Kelsey cooperated with Rev. W. C. Cook, a pastor of the First Baptist Church in Clovis, who established a Baptist mission at the rancheria in 1909, after the Baptist youth of the San Joaquin Valley purchased an additional forty-acre ranch for a mission station. Some of my extended family had earlier settled near there after white people forced them off traditional land. A few of their descendants continue to live at the "mission," known today as Big Sandy Rancheria.

Big Sandy's mission officials also successfully persuaded the Bureau of Indian Affairs to purchase one hundred sixty acres at Table Mountain, in the foothills near the San Joaquin River. This area, the ancestral home of the Dumna, had more recently been occupied by Nɨm and Chukchansi, who were displaced from other areas. Some of my extended family also settled there.

Although she was exposed to the teaching of the Presbyterian church for at least a decade, Grandma never accepted Christianity. All the while she was at the mission school, her parents and grandparents continued to teach her the Nɨm way of life and also told her to respect other people's ideas. So when I was about seven or eight years old and the preacher at the Presbyterian Mission Church came to our home across the way and invited Grandma to attend his church, she accepted. Almost every Sunday, she and Mom went to church while Gloria and I went to Sunday school. Grandma said that in order to get along with the white man we should learn about his God and Christ Jesus. I never accepted these ideas as anything more than information; Grandma and Grandpa were my teachers. It was lots of fun, though, swimming in their pool.

I remember when the teacher told us the story about a man named Noah, who built an ark to protect him, his family, and all of the animals from a great flood. I already knew about the great flood, from a story both Grandma and Grandpa told.

The Nɨm heard a sound of water hitting a shoreline. They kept hearing this sound for days. They wondered what it was, so they sent people to see. The people got to a place and saw a wall of water coming toward them. They hurried back to the rest of the people and said, "There is water coming. It will be here in a week." All the people started preparing food to take with them to the high country. They pounded acorn, berries, and seeds. They packed dry meat and took off for higher ground. People stayed to watch and send messages back to the people. The water kept coming and the people went higher and higher into the mountains. They reached the high-

est mountain. There they lived with the animals. They lived together for weeks upon weeks. The water receded and the Nɨm followed it back to their homes.

Mom says, "They [her ancestors] knew something was going to
happen so they made lots of acorn and took it when we all went to
the top, and when the water was gone we all went back home. My
Grandma said the ashes from their fires are still on the top of the
mountain."

During an exploration of the high country a few years ago, I went
to the top of that mountain, the highest point in our territory. I
walked about, in and out of narrow passages between huge boulders. I found a large fish carved on one of them. It appeared to be
very old. It was easy to imagine someone sitting there surrounded
by water, seeing the fish swimming by, and recording the event by
carving its image on the boulder. I found ashes, too, just as Great-
grandma Lizzie told Mom.

After Grandma had attended the Presbyterian service for several
years, one Sunday she told the preacher she wouldn't be back. He
asked why. She replied that for years she'd heard about a person
called God who could do so many things, a God she was to wor-
ship and ask for help. "I've never seen God or been aware of him,"
she added. "Every day I go outside and see the trees and flowers,
hear the wind, feel the sunshine or the rain or the snow. They talk
to me and answer my questions. They are strength when I need
them." We never returned.

As families continued to be fragmented, as more children were
taken to the Indian mission, a new effort began in 1915—to find
permanent homes for the Nɨm who lived west of the San Joaquin
River. Mr. Hood, Shinn, and John J. Terrell, a special federal Indian
agent, began looking for a permanent land base so as to remove the
Nɨm once and for all from the forest and put them on a reservation.
The Forest Service saw a reservation as a final settlement of its effort to remove the Indians still living within the Sierra National

Forest boundaries. The Presbyterian church was supportive because it would be in a better position to convert those Indians who continued to follow their "heathen" ways.

In California a reservation was the only logical solution to the landless Indians' problems, since the prevailing attitude was that Indians were not entitled to property rights and were trespassing on the public domain after they were deprived of squatter's rights to their settlements. In spite of their longevity at any one place, Indians could be removed, at will, by anyone.

"Rev. Hood and [his] wife insisted," Terrell wrote to the Commissioner of Indian Affairs in Washington, D.C., "that in the event of its purchase . . . most of these Indians living now too far away to send their children to school and those too far usually to regularily [sic] attend church services, would soon build their cottage homes thereon, that they might have these much needed advantages."[8]

Henry Coleman, a Nim who was living near North Fork, had one school-age child. He conducted a partial "Census of the Indians of Northfork [sic]," identifying ninety-four school-age children from thirty-nine families of both full and half degrees of Indian blood who lived in the vicinity. Several of my family members with school-age children were listed—my great-grandparents Jim Moore and Dick Pomona; Joseph Kinsman; Mike McDonald; Sam Pomona; Tom Harris; Housen Lavell; Frank Schulte; John Jackson; and Wilson Chepo.

On a Sunday in April 1916 about one hundred fifty of the two hundred Indians estimated by Dr. Hood as belonging to the North Fork area "band" met with Terrell at the conclusion of the church service. Those who attended agreed to support a reservation across from the mission as their permanent home.

A month later, on May 17, 1916, Aaron W. Frederick, the North Fork teacher, and his wife, Caroline E. Frederick, deeded to the federal government "for the use of the North Fork band of landless Indians" eighty-four acres located about one mile east of the mission. The purchase price was $550. My grandparents called this place Napisha´a. Non-Indians call it the North Fork Rancheria.

Mr. Hood, Terrell, and Shinn believed the Nɨm's so-called worthless land would impel the "poor and homeless Indians" to move to the North Fork Rancheria, and they were surprised when most of the eligible Nɨm didn't relocate. In July 1917 Maude Hart, a mission teacher, asked several families to build temporary housing at the rancheria, but they declined. "I have had such a time about these Indians," she wrote Terrell in October, "and now they have decided to go on to some U.S. Govt. land just outside of Mission, so don't want to go on 80 a. & after I got permission for them to go, and they were anxious for me to do so. . . . and now they have moved elsewhere."9

Discouraged, Terrell wrote the commissioner of Indian affairs at Washington, D.C.:

> Found the subdivision of the lands purchased for the village homes for the Indians not an easy one. It is difficult to get all the Indians entitled to an allotment on this land together at any one time, nor is it an easy matter to conclude who is justly entitled to one of these tentative subdivisions. . . . [T]he Indians should not be permitted to take possession of the land and establish themselves in a haphazard manner, according to their liking, for to do so almost always results in confusion, not infrequently proving more or less serious.10

My great-grandparents, Lizzie and Jim Moore, were typical of the relocation. By the late 1930s Great-grandma Lizzie's children were grown and her grandchildren were boarding at the mission. Grandma said that her mother missed her sister, Teeny, whose family—she, her husband, Jim Jackson, and their children—had already left their home at Tajiniu, near the San Joaquin River, to settle at Tɨpoki, about a mile west of Napisha´a, on land administered by the U.S. Forest Service.

Left to right: Lizzie Moore, carrying her granddaughter, Ethel Pomona, and her daughter Margaret Moore leave Sunday services at the North Fork Presbyterian Indian Mission in the early 1920s. (Author's collection)

Mom said her grandparents initially planned to live at Napishaˊa, "so they could all be together." She described Napishaˊa as beautiful rolling land with several good springs. Tall mature oak and pine trees grew everywhere, and the land was virtually clear of underbrush due to the occasional fires that slowly spread through the forest. One day, Mom said, her grandparents drove their horse-drawn wagon to Napishaˊa and chose a flat, tree-shaded spot near its western boundary as a place to build a house. When they returned soon afterward, they discovered that someone had cut down the trees. Then her Grandpa Jim dragged lumber behind his horse to build the house. When they returned, the lumber was burned up.

Great-grandma Lizzie decided they weren't welcome on the rancheria, so in the early 1940s she and her grandchildren moved in with her sister, Teeny. Great-grandpa Jim stayed at Peyakinu until his death in 1948. Up the road from our place, other families also moved to Tɨpoki rather than live at the rancheria.

Great-grandma Lizzie knew it was too crowded living in her sister's house. Grandpa John decided to help his mother. In the early 1940s he built her a small house closer to Cascadel Road but within easy walking distance of her sister's house. After Grandma Lizzie died in the mid-1940s, her daughter—Mom's Aunt Margaret and my grandma—who was at that time living in Coarsegold with her husband, Jim Bobb, came home to finish raising her now teenaged nieces and nephews.

Great-grandma Teeny's daughter, Annie Lewis (née Jackson), was working as a housekeeper for Frank Benedict, the Sierra National Forest supervisor at that time. When she explained to him the problems the Nɨm were having settling at Tɨpoki, Benedict issued Grandma Annie the first of several "free-use" permits so her family could continue to live there. Other families were also awarded permits, including Grandma, who received ten acres, and Grandpa, who received an adjacent five acres.

All the permit land was later transferred from the Sierra National Forest to the Bureau of Indian Affairs, enabling the families to apply for public domain allotment status under the Forest Allotment Act of June 25, 1910. Unfortunately, when their permitted land became allotted land, Grandma's share was reduced to seven and one-half acres and Grandpa received nothing; another family was awarded the balance of their shares. Grandma was unforgiving. The Tɨpoki allotments continue to be administered by the Bureau of Indian Affairs, as do a number of other public domain allotments in and around North Fork that were also awarded years ago.

Although it wasn't by their own choosing, after scores of years moving westward along the San Joaquin River our family finally had a secure land base. After Grandma's death in 1981 her allotment was divided between her heirs. Mom and I still have homes here, and Uncle Harvey recently returned.

Back to the mission. After the reservation was established, most parents continued to resist the mission's efforts to move them onto it, although some had moved closer to North Fork. Only twenty-four boarding students and three nonboarding students were enrolled at the mission school in 1918.

The mission school, well established and fully equipped, operated in spite of these problems. Kindergarten through eighth grade students were taught the usual course of instruction, according to a report in a publication of the Women's Board of Home Missions of the Presbyterian Church. Everyone studied the Bible; instrumental music and household arts were taught; and there was even instruction in gardening. According to another report that year, "In the home life and work she [the Indian girl] shows to good advantage, readily adapting herself to the 'white way' of doing things. . . . [E]ternal vigilance and constant drilling produce results. . . . Great changes . . . is coming into the lives of these people and that consecrated devotion is winning many victories over ignorance and superstition."[12]

In 1924 the four outlying schools near North Fork voted to consolidate with the newly opened North Fork Elementary School that was built east of Willow Creek at the outskirts of town. After mission personnel decided it was advantageous for its boarding school students to attend public school, they were bused there. Any Nɨm parents who still lived a distance from North Fork and whose children had attended an outlying school were now expected to enroll their children in the North Fork school. The mission began boarding those children, too, increasing the number of boarders to forty-six girls by 1930. Boys were finally boarded a year later, after another dormitory was built. In the early 1930s, after the girls' dormitory burned to the ground, new mission buildings were built on the west side of Cascadel Road.

Mom and Aunt Ethel were young children when they lived with their Grandma Lizzie and Grandpa Jim at Peyakinu after their mother, Emma, died. Soon afterward, another daughter, Daisy Moore Punkin, whose Nɨm name was Chuwanu, died in an accident. Her sons, Herb and Harvey, also spent time with their grandparents. Mom said missionaries came there one day and took the girls to board at the mission. Her memories are vivid: of being whipped by teachers when she spoke the Nɨm language, the only one she knew, and of loneliness for her family as she tried to learn a foreign culture. Looking back, though, Mom says it was good for her to be there, to learn how to cook the white man's food, to sew, and to do the things the white children were learning at their homes. The memories of other family members, particularly some of the men, are less kind. "It was a concentration camp," one uncle said.

The missionaries were pleased to finally see the old ways disappearing, as some of the Indian community began to embrace the Christian lifestyle. They abandoned their cedar bark houses for frame ones, opened bank accounts, and sought employment from white people. The Forest Service cooperated with the mission by hiring some of the boys to work for them. Girls worked locally as housemaids or if they moved to larger cities, as maids and nannies there. How sad that none were encouraged to continue their education at schools of higher learning, to become professional people, as some of their non-Indian friends did. It is a continuing problem today.

The mission closed in the early 1950s. By then many Nɨm families had relocated nearer to North Fork. The boarding school was no longer necessary to assure the children's continuing education at the North Fork Elementary School.

When Congress passed the Rancheria Act of 1958 authorizing the termination of the federal-trust relationship of rancherias, Susan Johnson was the only person living on the eighty-acre North Fork Indian Rancheria. On April 29, 1960, the rancheria reverted to fee patent public land. In the early 1980s, however, Mrs. Johnson's heirs, identifying themselves as the "Mono Indian Tribe," successfully sued the federal government to have the North Fork Indian Rancheria reinstated. The rancheria receives an annual budget award from the Bureau of Indian Affairs to conduct its affairs, but because the real property was recognized as a trust allotment on

which only Mrs. Johnson's heirs could live, other Nɨm are pre-
cluded from living there. The rancheria periodically enrolls new
members from those Nɨm who can prove descendancy from North
Fork Mono ancestors.

Twice during this century, by awarding California's Indians
nominal amounts for the land taken from their ancestors when the
government failed to ratify the 1851 treaties, the government has
attempted to redress that wrong. Grandma Annie recalled that two
lawyers, Kellet and Johnson, came to the North Fork area when she
was a young woman (probably in the mid-1920s) to encourage the
Nɨm to sign "Indian rolls" so the federal government could deter-
mine who was entitled to land compensation. The lawyers hosted
a big party in North Fork with "lots of eats," Grandma Annie said.
"Everybody signed."

In 1928 Congress passed the California Indian Jurisdictional Act
authorizing the state's attorney general to sue the federal government in the court of claims to compensate any and all claims made
by Indians against the United States. The unratified treaties and
the failed reservation system were the basis for a net judgment in
1944 of $12,029,099, and amount equal to $1.25 an acre.

In 1946 Congress approved a second bill called the Indian
Claims Commission Act which permitted any Indian tribe to sue
the government for past actions. California's Indians, again basing
their claims on the failed treaties, were among 152 plaintiff groups.
Between 1950 and 1956 major hearings were held throughout the
country, but a final determination favoring California's Indians
wasn't made until 1959. It was another nine years before President
Lyndon B. Johnson signed a bill providing $29 million in com-
pensation to 50,000 verified descendants who had lived on the
treatied lands. This time the land was valued at 47¢ per acre.
Grandma couldn't recall the amount she received, but Grandma
Annie remembered that her share of that judgment was $300.

After the rancheria was created and as the years passed, public
officials began to identify Nɨm who continued to live either on

public domain allotments or elsewhere near North Fork as North
Fork Mono. My grandparents never identified themselves as North
Fork Mono. Sometimes, if asked what tribe they were from, they'd
reply, "Nɨm from the San Joaquin River." Other times I'd hear
Grandma say, "I'm Nɨm from Tɨpoki." In recent years, other people
have stopped referring to themselves as North Fork Mono and are
identifying themselves as Nɨm. Perhaps some day everyone will
call themselves by their original tribal identity, Nɨm, including
governmental entities and the anthropological community.

CHAPTER ELEVEN

WHEN IT'S COLD

When daytime temperatures drop so low the few leaves still dangling from tree branches begin to fall crackling to the ground; when flakes of snow dance earthward and water becomes so cold a patterned quilt of ice blankets the lakes; when Bear begins to yawn and seeks shelter for her long winter nap and Buzzard flies south; "when it's cold," it's to'wano, a cycle in the unbroken circle of life. Non-Indians call this time winter. Mom recalls much heavier snowfalls when she was a child than there are now. Grandma said there are cycles to life; the heavy snowfalls will return.

On bright sunny days Mom enjoys the out-of-doors, snuggled down in a protected spot near the trees or by a sunny wall preparing her basket material, making baskets, or making soap brushes. Perhaps she'll clean acorn or do one of her favorite pastimes, solving a crossword puzzle.

Years ago, when it was storming, the family would stay inside their cedar bark houses, playing games or, now that Rattlesnake was fast asleep and wouldn't hurt anyone if stories were told, listening to the grandparents tell stories, the same ones that have been shared from generation to generation. At those times when the storms abated, women left the warm comfort of their homes to gather basket materials, fashion new tools, or repair the old ones.

When I was growing up, on cold winter nights we'd sit near the wood-burning stove, listening to Grandpa and Grandma tell us stories. Those evenings are among my happiest childhood memories.

Once, throughout to'wano the men continued to hunt for fresh meat and fished the streams that weren't frozen over. I listened with rapt attention as Grandpa told us his favorite hunting story.

The land was snowing and Coyote and Mouse were sitting in a cave. Inside a fire was glowing and warm. Coyote said, "I will go and kill some jackrabbits when the snow gets so high." He told this to his nephews, Mice. So Mice said, "All right." Coyote went to sleep and Mice were afraid he would eat them. So they decided to play a trick on him. They waited and waited. The snow got higher and higher. They woke their uncle up and said, "It's time to go hunting." Coyote got up and went outside. He sank into the snow and couldn't get out. In the snow he yelled to his nephews, "I'm going to kill you when I get out." His nephews got scared and ran away. They got a stick from their fire and left, running on top of the snow. They were going to where Mountain Sheep lived. Mountain Sheep lived on top of a high mountain inside a cave. They got to where Mountain Sheep stayed. By this time their uncle, Coyote, got out of the snow and went inside his house. There he waited until the snow melted and got hard. He went after his nephews, Mice, and tracked them. He followed them to the mountain. His nephews, Mice, had reached Mountain Sheep and told them they were freezing cold. Mountain Sheep told them to climb into their stomachs through their butts and they would become warm. So they did and got warm. They started to feel hungry so they started eating Mountain Sheep. They started biting their stomachs and killed Mountain Sheep. Their uncle, Coyote, was walking around down under the mountain. He yelled, "I can't climb. Throw me some meat. I'm starving." "No, we can't. We'll throw you some bones." So they threw him some bones.

After he ate he walked around along the roads and dropped white bones which he ate. That's why you see white bones today along the roads.

Beads were often strung during to´wano. Clam and olivella shells were traded from Pacific Coast tribes. Sometimes the family even traveled "to the west at the big salty water," as Grandma described the Pacific Ocean, to gather shells. Since time was meaningless, the journey, by foot or on horseback, was relaxed as the family camped along the way.

Beads were made by piercing a hole in small pieces of shell with an obsidian drill, stringing the shell on milkweed cord, and then rolling the string back and forth on sandstone until they were a uniform shape. Soapstone beads were made the same way; sometimes they were even incorporated into the tanned deerskin clothing that was usually made during to´wano.

In the old days beads were money, used as a medium of exchange. Their value was measured in lengths from the fingertips to the elbow, and they were used to purchase baskets, horses, and whatever else was available.

Glass beads were introduced to California's Indians in the 1800s by the Hudson Bay Trading Company. Early explorers and trappers were the first to trade red and blue glass beads to Indians near our territory, who then traded to us. Later, trappers brought glass beads directly to our territory. They eventually replaced shell beads.

I sometimes find shell or glass beads behind my home at Tɨpoki, where Nɨm lived long before my family and others moved here. Grandma said a grassy knoll behind the house, where there is a large granite outcropping covered with holes for pounding acorns and seeds, was once a gathering place for trading.

Many Nɨm still do beadwork. They fashion ornaments for jewelry and hair pieces and add beads to wallets, belt buckles, and whatever else strikes their fancy. Glass beads are usually bought at intertribal powwows or at hobby stores.

During the cold days of to wano women ranged near and far gathering material for basketry. While a woman was gathering seeds a long, long time ago, she discovered the strongest material for making baskets.

A woman was gathering seeds down in the valley. Her husband went to sleep under a tree as the woman kept picking seeds and putting them into a big basket. She went out a little farther to look for more seeds. Her husband was still asleep when a huge bird came. He was Niniyociti. He came and picked her husband up with its wing and put her husband on its back. Niniyociti dropped a feather where he had picked the man up. Niniyociti flew higher and higher with the man on his back, singing a song: "Pachanakii, howananakii, pachanakii, howananakii, chu chu chu, chu chu chu" ["When I get home we'll drink water"]. On and on it flew, higher and higher. The man was crying because he missed his wife. His tears got the bird wet. The bird tired because of his wet feathers. The bird was thirsty and when they got up to where the sky ended, went through a hole. He told his passenger that they would drink water when they arrived where he stayed. The Indians that stayed back there were Miwok Indians. Niniyociti had many people there already. He would kill the Indians and drink their blood. These Indians heard the bird coming and starting singing, "Haki hakont, haki hakont, haki hakont," and when it reached the house they told the man not to drink his water because it was blood. They told him to drink the good water over there on the other side. The man was so tired he barely walked over to get a drink. After he drank the Indians told him to get that sharp bladed grass and cut the bird's head off. The Indians told him to wait until he went to get a drink. The man waited until the bird went to drink his water. The bird bent his neck over and when he did that the man cut his neck. All the people were free now. The bird had captured them and kept them there. They were happy and gave a feast and had a good time playing handgames and singing. This went on all night. The man was tired

and went to sleep after watching the handgames. He awoke the next
morning. The Indians asked the man if he wanted to go home. This
was done because he had freed them. The man said, "Yes." So they
tried to find something to reach the earth. They tried bark, milkweed, redbud, and leatherwood, and whatever they had. But all the
material they tried would break when it touched the earth. They
tried sedge grass root and it didn't break so they sent him home on
this string. They told him to jerk the string when he reached bottom. He reached bottom and jerked on the string and the Indians
pulled it up into the sky. He went back to where his wife was, but
she was gone. He started home to Siyakinu. All this time his wife
was crying and she cut her hair as the old-timers did. He arrived
home and she was so happy to see him she cried again. She told
him she found a feather and thought that something bad had happened to him. But now he was home and she was happy.

—as told by Grandma

Grandma said that was a good lesson we learned, when the man
was kidnapped by the Niniyociti: to use the white root of the sedge
grass to make our baskets strong.

Since glass and metal have replaced the need to weave baskets
for daily use, the handful of women who still make them usually
weave only twined work baskets or baby baskets; they seldom coil
baskets. Grandma used to say, "If you don't use something it will
rot." So our family continues to use most of its baskets for their intended purpose. Mom cooks in her *apo*, a cooking basket woven by
her Grandma Lizzie, and stores acorn in a large coiled basket that
Grandma Lizzie also wove years ago. I store bird feathers in finely
woven small baskets once made to store trinkets, including a del-
icately woven twined basket shaped like a shoe, woven by Great-
grandma Kitty. We still gather grasses and mushrooms in a
chamaiya. The twined sifters—we call them *timoiya*—and seed
beaters are still used occasionally. Grandma was so generous that
our family doesn't have all of the baskets we once did. When she

Emma Moore at Peyakinu in about 1919. She is holding a twined acorn basket. On the ground, *left to right,* are a winnowing basket, two coiled cooking or serving baskets, a burden basket used for carrying loads, and a sifting basket. (Author's collection)

went visiting, she'd fill a basket with pine nuts to give to a friend, especially during the Christmas holiday season.

Young girls learned how to weave baskets in the old days by watching their mother and grandmothers. Mom watched her Grandma Lizzie, but because she was at the mission school she didn't actually begin making baskets until she was a mature woman.

Basket weavers still gather material primarily during to´wano, when the young, slender shoots that develop in cold weather are pliable. Although basketry is considered women's work, the whole family used to be included in the gathering process. I've gone with Mom to help her cut branches and dig roots, and had a grand time. Sometimes if we're out gathering mushrooms during winter, or even in spring, Mom or Aunt Ethel will see some material and everything comes to a halt while they cut their sticks.

Mom usually begins gathering redbud sticks when these trees are dormant in December and continues into February. She says the color is a deeper red then, better for her baskets. Although the natural-colored sourberry sticks are also gathered during to´wano, they can be cut throughout spring, but then the twigs and leaves have to be removed. Metal knives have replaced the obsidian blades once used for this task. The sticks were easily transported by tying them together in small bunches to carry like a purse by hand, or by tying them together in larger bunches to carry as a load on the back. The tying straps were made with bark stripped off a branch from the flannel bush. Mom still does this sometimes, but sometimes she uses store-bought twine.

The material must be cleaned before it can be used. On a mild winter day Mom often sits outside in the sunshine skillfully peeling bark off her redbud or sourberry sticks with a sharp knife or splitting unpeeled redbud sticks in two by clamping one end of the stick in her teeth and skillfully splitting it in half from one end to the other. She divides the sticks into bunches by size, evenly distributed by length and diameter, and wraps them in cloth to use later. Because basket material is difficult to work with when it dries out, it must be soaked in water beforehand. In the old days women buried the material in moist earth. Mom soaks hers in a pail of water.

Work baskets, such as seed beaters and winnowers, are made with redbud or sourberry sticks. The bark is split and woven together, sometimes with the bark reversed to create a lighter, cream-colored pattern. The edges are bound with chaparral. Skill is necessary to achieve the specific shapes for specific uses.

Water was stored in a twined basket made of split redbud, somewhat conical in shape, with a flared mouth. It looks like a canteen. This basket was sealed by first applying pitch from the bull pine on the outside, then putting hot coals inside and immediately shaking the basket vigorously to draw the pitch from outside in. By plug-

ging the opening with a cork made from either milkweed fiber or
wild oat grass, water wouldn't spill out.

Sometimes the Nɨm traded for water bottles with the Paiutes.
Mom doesn't recall seeing her Grandma weave one. When we
married, my wife brought a water bottle to the family. It was woven
years ago by Refugia Williams, who was a Nɨwɨ, a tribe identified
today as Kawaiisu. They speak a language very similar to ours. She
was born near Ballarat in the Panamint Valley of the great Mojave
Desert and lived for many years near Kernville in the southern
Sierra Nevada. We have quite a few of her baskets.

Willow tree branches were also gathered and split like the redbud. They were used to weave twined cooking baskets and were
sometimes decorated with interwoven redbud or bracken fern. The
binding was redbud. Grandma's cooking basket was made by her
mother, Lizzie, and although it is worn and frayed, repaired by
Grandma using pieces of string, it is still usable.

Coiled baskets were always used for storing ekibe. They are usually made with material from three plants but are rarely made anymore. The foundation of a coiled basket is bunchgrass. It's gathered
near moist places. The white root of sedge grass gives the basket
its creamy color. White root is dug from spring to early summer,
near banks of creeks or streams, and stored for later use. Although
sedge grass grows in the mountains, the roots aren't as long as
those that grow in the San Joaquin Valley. Mom said her Grandma
Lizzie preferred to travel there for white root. So does Mom, but
it's increasingly difficult to obtain because private property own-
ers have closed most of the land. Peeled redbud bark provides a
design's red color. Bracken fern is also used for design. It, too, is
gathered at moist places in the mountains; but because its color is
brown, it's buried in mud to color it black. Most women now usually blacken the fern by putting it into a rusty can for a while.

Other coiled baskets include flat gambling trays, with just a hint
of a lip to hold the dice, and trinket baskets. Some coiled baskets
had wide-flared tops, others were narrow or had bottlenecks

Lizzie and Jim Moore at Peyakinu, date unknown. Mrs. Moore is holding a coiled acorn cooking or serving basket in her left hand and a coiled trinket basket in her right hand. *Left to right:* A sifting basket, a twined storage basket, and three coiled cooking or serving baskets. (Author's collection)

woven to the top. Ceremonial baskets were also coiled. In the old days the women wove quail topknots around the edge of this basket; occasionally a woman still does.

Many designs were woven into our basketry. Some were unique to the weaver; others were universal. Designs were not drawn in advance but were woven into the basket as it was made. The rattlesnake diamond pattern is typical of the acorn storage basket, but human figures—sometimes hand-in-hand, male and female alike—were also used. There were other designs: stair steps, butterflies, pine trees, racer snakes, water snakes, rain, centipedes, stinkbugs, and deer hooves.

Grandpa Willie's sister, Nancy Pomona Sherman, wove the eye

Lizzie Moore carries her granddaughter, Ethel Pomona, in a baby basket, as she and her husband, Jim Moore, walk in the early 1920s from Mrs. Moore's sister's home at Tɨpoki to Sunday services at the North Fork Presbyterian Indian Mission. (Author's collection)

of the yellow jacket into a gathering basket. You might wonder how anyone could get close enough to observe a yellow jacket's eye. When I was a kid, Grandpa took me to visit the yellow jackets' home. We went early one morning when, he said, the yellow jackets are still sluggish from their night's sleep, and we could get so close that we would stare into the wasp's eyes as he stared back. Grandpa was right.

Baby baskets are supposed to be woven by an infant's paternal grandmother. So few women weave now that these baskets are usually bought from the few weavers who are left. In the old days a baby basket was often leaned on a tree or against a rock while its mother was gathering. The basket hoop not only shaded the baby's face but also protected the baby if the basket tipped over.

Peeled sourberry sticks and peeled redbud sticks are the baby basket's framework. The split redbud sticks are woven in and out of the sourberry sticks, and a finish binding of young chaparral shoots is woven around the edge. Sometimes reversed redbud bark is used. There are actually two baby baskets. In the old days, before the infant was born, its paternal grandmother wove a basket with a simple band or hoop attached to the upper front of the basket. She also made a finger-weave binding of milkweed fibers to secure the infant in its basket; yarn is used today. The newborn baby stayed in its first basket for several months, snug and secure while the mother went about her daily chores. Even today one seldom sees a crying, fussing Indian baby in its basket. They sleep peacefully; when awake, they're smiling and cooing. About a month after its birth the infant's family gathers with gifts for the baby and watches the paternal grandmother pull the baby through the hoop, from top to bottom. As the grandmother pulls the baby through, she gives it a Nɨm name. Although we are now given American names at birth, family names are still occasionally given to a new infant. Because my grandson's father is a non-Indian, in the absence of a paternal Indian grandmother Mom pulled Anthony through his first basket and named him Sakɨma.

When the baby was about a year old and had outgrown its first basket, it was given a second larger basket that had a larger hoop to provide shade. Sometimes shells or beads were hung from the hoop; as they swayed gently in the breeze, they made a comforting sound. This basket has distinct designs: a boy's basket has a straight diagonal design to ensure his arrow will fly straight and true when he hunts. A girl's basket is stitched with a diamond-shaped pattern, ensuring her own ability to weave beautiful designs. In the old days, when the baby outgrew its second basket, it was hung in the branches of a bull pine tree to ensure that it would grow as straight and tall as the tree. The basket was left to decay naturally. Most mothers now keep the baby's basket.

Throughout to'wano the men continued to hunt for fresh meat and fish the streams. The days passed. But one day, after leaving the warmth of home, the early morning air wouldn't be quite so

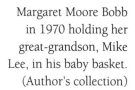

Margaret Moore Bobb
in 1970 holding her
great-grandson, Mike
Lee, in his baby basket.
(Author's collection)

cold and one's breath wouldn't be visible. As the sun rose in the sky a new sound was heard, the drip, drip, drip of melting ice. "When the ice starts melting," Grandma said, "puhiduwa is just around the corner." Nighttime is shorter, the days are longer, the time of renewal is almost here.

"Hau, hau, hau." Even today, the song of Hauhauna, Goose, still calls me outside. He flies with other geese in formation on their cyclical migration north. Look! There they are, high in the sky. Watch Hauhauna as he dips at the horizon, disappearing in his knowledgeable flight northward. To'wano is almost ended.

Soon afterward, if you look skyward you might see the turkey buzzards, arriving in paired flight as they seek suitable nesting trees for their soon-to-be-hatched babies. Grandma sang Buzzard's song this way:

> Up high I fly where it is cold.
> I go north in April where it is cool.
> When the rain and snow hit my bald head
> I go south where it is warm.

CHAPTER TWELVE

EPILOGUE

The cycle is complete. As much as it is possible as the twentieth century ends, my family lives as we have always lived since all the animals gathered at Chu:wani and painted themselves with colors of the rainbow, populating the world.

The Nɨm are now a minority race in the land of our forefathers, pummeled and pushed by actions and rhetoric that sometimes seem to be insurmountable. Very few children speak the Nɨm language; they have little knowledge of the old ways. Some Nɨm have embraced ideas from other Indian cultures. Others seek political answers to today's challenges. And still others have turned to the public education system to reintroduce the Nɨm language and culture to the children. Many concerned non-Indians bemoan the disappearance of the Nɨm culture.

Grandma's admonition sustains me. "Aishupa´, Gaylen," she whispers. "Don't worry. It's OK." Thanks to her example and Grandpa's, I know that nothing ends, all of life goes on, they are still here, all of the old people are still here in other forms, continuing to teach us, if we will only listen.

It is still a land of startling contrasts. High in the fastness of the central Sierra Nevada, on a clear day a bright blue sky mantles the land. During stormy weather, wild cloud formations hug the peaks as a black sky darkens the landscape, and a cacophonous serenade of thunder breaks over one peak, rebounds to another and another and another, while lightning streaks across the sky creating a magnificent light show unduplicated by humankind. Spectacular granite domes thrust upward, towering mountains encircle scattered meadows bordered by ancient trees: there are coniferous pines and cedars and deciduous oaks that have survived the onslaught of over a century of domination by others.

But, although the San Joaquin River still flows through this splendid country, it no longer tumbles swiftly, freely, down through deep canyons from the highest reaches of the Sierra Nevada. Concrete and earthen dams impede its natural flow to the San Joaquin Valley, and virtually no free-flowing water remains so that it can continue northwestward, year-round.

My great-great-great-grandparents lived year-round in these mountains in 1851, at a large rolling meadow they called Cha:tiniu. Their peace was shattered in early spring. Some years later they moved away. Cha:tiniu is all but forgotten. Cattle graze there now, but this place is called Logan Meadow. It's a privately owned place surrounded by the Sierra National Forest near Mammoth Pool, about forty-five miles east of North Fork. There is no evidence of the Nïm who lived there, except for a large collection of artifacts displayed in a store that sells food and sundries to the thousands of people who visit yearly.

On a pleasant summer day in the early 1990s, while scores of tourists boated on the water impounded by Mammoth Pool Dam or sullied the nearby streams and forest trails, I picnicked with my wife at the edge of the meadow that was Cha:tiniu, watching cattle graze peacefully where my ancestors' cedar bark houses once dotted the landscape. I was absorbed by private daydreams and visions.

After a while, I left.

My story is over. The calendar says it has been spring for over seven weeks. Snow covers the mountains above Tɨpoki today. It has been raining intermittently for weeks, one of the wettest winters in memory. Springlike weather has yet to arrive. It was as cold last night as in winter. Rattlesnake sleeps soundly. Grandpa and Grandma, all of my ancestors, are always with me.

LINGUISTIC
METHODOLOGY

In the 1970s, when I realized that many Nɨm words were disappearing from lack of use or because of cultural change, my grandparents, Mom, and others, all of whom were fluent speakers, aided me in reducing our oral language to writing.

I referred to Sidney Lamb's dissertation, "Northfork Mono Grammar," which uses various symbols universally accepted by linguists. But when I wrote words with his system, a test group was unable to read them correctly. For example:

1. When the test group saw the letter *j* in a word, they used the sound in "jump," instead of the *y* sound as in "you." I use the letter *y* for that sound. (See Lamb, page 39.)

2. The test group had difficulty understanding Lamb's use of the letter *c* for the "ch" sound. I use the letters *ch* for that sound. (See Lamb, page 49.)

3. The test group had a hard time with Lamb's use of the letter *x* for the hard *k* as in "kiss." I use the letter *k* for clarity. (See Lamb, page 47.)

I worked with Evan Norris, who was a linguistics major in the M.A. program at California State University, Fresno, when I was an undergraduate student there. We devised what I believe is a simpler vowel and consonant system. Lists of words were given to five Nɨm speakers and five non-Nɨm speakers. This test group had little difficulty understanding our system; all were able to read the words. Norris's thesis, "A Syntactic Sketch of Mono," uses the system we devised. For several years I wrote and published an annual calendar in the Nɨm language which used this linguistic system. I've been told it was easily understood.

NOTES

CHAPTER 1. INTRODUCTION
1. Kroeber, *Handbook of the Indians of California*, 584.

CHAPTER 3. THE FIRST STRANGERS
1. Cook, *Colonial Expeditions to the Interior of California, Central Valley*, 251.

2. Coarsegold Historical Society, *As We Were Told*, 369. All quotations in this paragraph are from this source.

3. Coarsegold Historical Society, *As We Were Told*, 369.

4. Bunnell, *Discovery of the Yosemite*, 61.

5. Shinn, "Old Man Chepo," 622.

6. Fremont, *Memoirs of My Life*, 39–40. All quotations in this paragraph are from this source.

CHAPTER 5. SPRING, WHEN UNINVITED GUESTS BRING GIFTS OF DEATH
1. Crampton, *The Discovery of Yosemite and the Mariposa Indian War*, 64. Robert Eccleston's original leatherbound diaries are in the Bancroft Library, University of California, Berkeley.

2. Kinsman, "Reminiscences," *Madera County Magazine*, 1915, 1.

3. Cunningham's recollections are in the James Savage Collection, Yosemite Research Library. All quotations in this paragraph are from the same source.

4. Bunnell, *Discovery of the Yosemite in 1851*, 15.

5. Ibid., 24.

6. Coarsegold Historical Society, *As We Were Told*, 59–60.

7. Burney to Hutchings, 20 March 1885, James Savage Collection, Yosemite Research Library.

8. Unidentified correspondent in *Daily Alta Californian*, 23 April 1851, Microfilm, Yosemite Research Library. Emphasis added.

9. Crampton, *The Discovery of Yosemite and the Mariposa Indian War*, 64.

10. Bunnell, *Discovery of the Yosemite in 1851*, 111.

11. Bowling to Savage, 11 June 1851, *Daily Alta Californian*, Microfilm, Yosemite Research Library. Bowling's quotes in the next three pages are from the same source.

12. Bunnell, *Discovery of the Yosemite in 1851*, 129.

13. Treaty of 29 April 1851 between several San Joaquin Valley tribes and the U.S. government. National Archives, Washington, D.C.

14. Latta, *Handbook of the Yokuts Indians*, 663.

15. Ibid., 665.

16. Unidentified correspondent, 10 May 1851, *Daily Alta Californian*, Microfilm, Yosemite Research Library.

17. Bunnell, *Discovery of the Yosemite in 1851*, 81.

18. *Daily Alta Californian*, Microfilm, Yosemite Research Library.

19. Latta, *Handbook of the Yokuts Indians*, 662.

20. Ibid., 666.

21. Heizer and Almquist, *The Other Californians*, 85.

22. H. W. Wessell report, Department of the Pacific, Fort Tejon Collection, Beale Memorial Library, Bakersfield, California.

23. Russell, "Geography of the Mariposa Indian War," 71.

24. Kinsman, 5 April 1893, Diary. A typescript copy of Kinsman's diary is at the Sierra Mono Museum, North Fork, California.

25. Latta, *Handbook of the Yokuts Indians*, 666.

26. Brewer, *Up and Down California in 1860–1864*, 539.

27. Ibid., 540.

28. Ibid., 546.

CHAPTER 6. ENJOYING LIFE DURING PUHIDUWA

1. Dorsey, *Indians of the Southwest*, 212.

2. Ibid.

CHAPTER 8. THE WARM DAYS OF SUMMER BRING SETTLERS

1. June English Collection, Madden Library, California State University, Fresno.

2. Ibid.

3. Ibid.

4. Microfilm records, U.S. Department of the Interior, Bureau of Land Management, Sacramento.

5. Noble, "A Day With the Mono Indians," 43.

6. Boothe, "The Personal Narrative of Roy Boothe," 11.

CHAPTER 9. WHEN DAYS TURN COOL

1. C. Hart Merriam Collection, "Nim" field notes, MSS. 80/18C, The Bancroft Library, Berkeley.

2. Muir, My First Summer in the Sierra, 218–19.

3. Dulce Tully Rose interview conducted by June English, 5 November 1979, June English Collection, Madden Library, University of California, Fresno.

4. Kinsman, "Reminiscences," 1.

5. Gene Tully interview conducted by June English, no date, June English Collection, Madden Library, Fresno.

6. Dulce Tully Rose interview conducted by June English, 5 November 1979.

CHAPTER 10. THE CHURCH, THE FOREST SERVICE, AND CHANGE

1. Kinsman, 13 June 1914, Diary.

2. Mrs. George Teaford's undated reminiscence, Historical Collection, North Fork branch, Madera County Library.

3. Noble to "Miss Fraser," 8 September 1903, Historical Collection, Presbyterian Historical Society.

4. Ibid.

5. Ibid.

6. Mrs. George Teaford's undated reminiscence, Historical Collection, North Fork branch, Madera County Library.

7. Kelsey, "Report to the Commissioner of Indian Affairs, Washington, D.C.," 12.

8. Terrell to Commissioner of Indian Affairs, Department of the Interior, Bureau of Indian Affairs, Sacramento, 4 April 1916, Archives, Bureau of Indian Affairs, Sacramento.

9. Hart to Terrell, 21 October 1917, Archives, Bureau of Indian Affairs, Sacramento.

10. Terrell to Commissioner of Indian Affairs, Department of the Interior, Bureau of Indian Affairs, Sacramento, 11 November 1917, Archives, Bureau of Indian Affairs, Sacramento.

11. "Nutshell Items," undated report of the Women's Board of Home Missions, no page numbers, Historical Collection, Presbyterian Historical Society.

BIBLIOGRAPHY

ARCHIVES AND COLLECTIONS

Beale Memorial Library, Kern County Library, Bakersfield, California.

Vernon Brooks Collection. Madden Library, California State University, Fresno.

Bureau of Indian Affairs. Archives. U.S. Department of the Interior, Sacramento, California.

California Indian Collection. North Fork Branch, Madera County Library, North Fork, California.

Eccleston, Robert. Diaries, vols. 5 and 6 (1851, 1852). The Bancroft Library, University of California, Berkeley.

June English Collection. Madden Library, California State University, Fresno.

Fort Tejon Collection. Beale Memorial Library, Bakersfield, California.

"Fresno Division, California Fish and Game Commission Records, Fish Stocking, 1870–1915." Archives. Minarets Ranger District, Sierra National Forest, North Fork, California.

Kinsman, Joseph. Diary of Joseph Kinsman. Sierra Mono Museum, North Fork, California.

Madden Library. Special Collections. California State University, Fresno.

Madera County Library. California Room. Madera, California.

Madera County Planning Department. Maps and Survey Notes, Survey Office. Madera, California.

Manley, Burnice. "The History of North Fork." Historical Archives. North Fork: Madera County Library, March 1966.

Mariposa History Library, Mariposa, California.

Merriam, C. Hart. "Genealogical Data, Mono Indians." Unpublished notes. The Bancroft Library, University of California, Berkeley.

————. "Monache Sierra Tribes, Field Notes, 1902–1930." Unpublished notes of the Mono culture. Cataloged no. X/23d/P, 4. The Bancroft Library, University of California, Berkeley.

————. "Nim." Field notes. Catalog no. MSS. 80/180C, October 5, 1902. C. Hart Merriam Collection. The Bancroft Library, University of California, Berkeley.

————. "Nim—'Mono' of North Fork Joaquin." MS. Catalog no. MSS. 80/18C. C. Hart Merriam Collection. Bancroft Library, University of California, Berkeley. October 4, 1902.

Minarets Ranger District. Archives. Sierra National Forest, North Fork, California.

North Fork Branch, Madera County Library. Historical Collection. North Fork, California.

Oakhurst Branch, Madera County Library. Historical Collection. Oakhurst, California.

James Savage Collection. Yosemite Research Library, Yosemite, California.

Sierra Mono Museum. Archives. North Fork, California.

Sierra National Forest. Archives. Supervisor's Office, Clovis, California.

Presbyterian Historical Society. Historical Collection. Philadelphia, Pennsylvania.

Stammerjohna, George R. "Historical Sketch of Millerton Lake State Recreation Area." Archives. Sierra National Forest, Clovis, n.d.

Thrall, B., A. H. Gayton, and Edward W. Gifford. "Northfork Mono Field Notes." 1918. Unpublished and uncataloged. The Bancroft Library, University of California, Berkeley.

Tully, Gene. "The First United States Forest Service Ranger Called: Indian Foresters." N.d. Archives. Sierra National Forest, Minarets Ranger District.

U.S. Department of the Interior. Bureau of Land Management. Map Section. Sacramento, California.

Yosemite Research Library, Yosemite, California.

BOOKS, ARTICLES, AND REPORTS

Anderson, George, W. H. Ellison, Robert F. Heizer. *Treaty Making and Treaty Rejection by the Federal Government in California, 1850–1852.* Socorro, New Mex.: Ballena Press, 1978.

Bethel, Rosalie, Paul Kroskrity, Christopher Loether, and Gregory A. Reinherdt. *A Practical Dictionary of Western Mono.* Los Angeles: American Indian Studies Center, University of California, 1984.

Boothe, Roy. "The Personal Narrative of Roy Boothe, Forest Supervisor." Clovis, Calif.: Historical Archives, Sierra National Forest, 1940.

Boyd, William Harland. *A California Middle Border.* Richardson, Texas: Havilah Press, 1972.

Brewer, William H. *Up and Down California in 1860–1864.* Edited by Francis P. Farquhar. New Haven: Yale University Press, 1930.

Bunnell, Lafayette Houghton, M.D. *Discovery of the Yosemite in 1851.* Los Angeles: G. W. Gerlicher, 1911. Reprint Golden, Colo.: Outbooks, 1980.

Bureau of Indian Affairs, U.S. Department of the Interior. Indian Office Files: "Tribal Reservations and Rancherias." Sacramento, 1916–17.

———. *Report of the California Indian Task Force.* Sacramento. October 1984.

Camp, Charles Lewis. *Kit Carson in California.* San Francisco: California Historical Society, 1922.

Carson, Christopher. *Kit Carson's Own Story of His Life.* Santa Fe: New Mexican Publishing Corp., 1955.

Caruthers, William. *Loafing Along Death Valley Trails.* Ontario, Calif.: Death Valley Publishing Co., 1951.

Clingan, Helen, and Forest Clingan. *Oak to Pine to Timberline.* Fresno: Pioneer, 1985.

Clough, Charles W., and William B. Secrest, Jr. *Fresno County: The Pioneer Years from the Beginning to 1900.* Fresno: Panorama West Books, 1984.

———. *Madera.* Madera: Madera County Diamond Jubilee Committee and the Madera County Historical Society, 1968.

Coarsegold Historical Society. *As We Were Told.* Coarsegold, Calif.: Coarsegold Historical Society, 1990.

Cook, S. F. *Colonial Expeditions to the Interior of California, Central Valley, 1800–1820.* Anthropological Records (University of California Press) 16, no. 6 (1960).

———. *The Epidemic of 1830–1833 in California and Oregon.* American Archaeology and Ethnology (University of California Press) 43, no. 3 (1955).

———. *Expeditions to the Interior of California, Central Valley of California, 1820–1840.* Anthropological Records (University of California Press) 20, no. 5 (1962).

Cossley-Batt, Jill L. *The Last of the California Rangers.* New York: Funk & Wagnalls, 1928.

Crampton, C. Gregory. *The Discovery of Yosemite and the Mariposa Indian War.* Salt Lake City: University of Utah Press, 1975.

————. "The Opening of the Mariposa Mining Region, 1849–1859." Ph.D. dissertation, University of California, Berkeley, 1941.

Curtis, Edward S. *The North American Indian* 15. Norwood, Mass.: Plimpton Press, 1926.

Dorsey, George A. *Indians of the Southwest.* n.p.: Passenger Department, Atchison Topeka & Santa Fe Railway System, 1903.

Essig, E. O. "The Value of Insects to the California Indians." *Scientific Monthly* 2 (1938): 181–86.

Forbes, Jack D. *Native Americans of California and Nevada.* Healdsburg, Calif.: Naturegraph, 1969.

Foster, Doris, and Clyde Foster. "One Hundred Years of History. Foster's Hogue Ranch." *Madera County Historian* 1, no. 4 (October 1961):1–8.

Fowler, Catherine S., and Nancy Peterson Walter. "Harvesting Pandora Moth Larvae with the Owens Valley Paiute." *Journal of California and Great Basin Anthropology* 7, no. 2 (1985):155–65.

Fremont, John C. *Memoirs of My Life, Including in the Narrative Five Journeys of Western Exploration During the Years 1842–3–4, 45–6–7, 48–9, 53–4.* Chicago: Clarke & Company, 1887.

————. *Report of the Exploring Expedition to the Rocky Mountains in the Year 1842, and to Oregon and Northern California in the Years 1843–'44.* Washington, D.C.: Blair and Rivers, 1845.

Garner, Van H. *The Broken Ring.* Tucson: Westernlore Press, 1982.

Gates, Doris. *North Fork.* New York: Viking Press, 1945.

Gayton, A. H. "The Ghost Dance of 1870 in South-Central California." *University of California Publications in American Archaeology and Ethnology* 28, no. 3 (1930):57–82.

Gifford, Edward Winslow. "Dichotomous Social Organization in South Central California." *University of California Publications in American Archaeology and Ethnology* 2, no. 5 (1916):291–96.

————. "The Northfork Mono." *University of California Publications in American Archaeology and Ethnology* 31, no. 2 (1932):15–65.

Hayne, Coe. *By-Paths to Forgotten Folks.* Philadelphia: Judson Press, 1921.

Heizer, Robert F., ed. *Federal Concern About Conditions of California Indians 1853* to 1913: Eight Documents. Publications in Archaeology, Ethnology, History, no. 13. Socorro, New Mex.: Ballena Press, 1979.

———. The Unratified Treaties of 1851–1852 Between the California Indians and the United States Government. Berkeley: University of California Archaeological Research Facility, 1972.

Heizer, Robert F., and Alan F. Almquist. The Other Californians: Prejudice and Discrimination Under Spain, Mexico, and the United States to 1920. Berkeley: University of California Press, 1971.

Heizer, Robert F., and Alfred L. Kroeber. "For Sale: California at 47 Cents Per Acre." Journal of California Anthropology 3, no. 2 (1965):38–65.

"Histories of Madera County Schools." Vol. 2. Madera: Madera County Department of Education, 1936.

Holland, Cecilia. The Bear Flag. Boston: Houghton Mifflin, 1990.

Hurtado, Albert L. Indian Survival on the California Frontier. New Haven: Yale University Press, 1988.

———. The Maidu and California Indian Policy, 1846–1855. Sacramento: California State University, Sacramento, 1974.

———. "Ranchos, Gold Mines and Rancherias: A Socioeconomic History of Indians and Whites in Northern California, 1821–1860." Ph.D. dissertation, University of California, Santa Barbara, 1981.

"Indians in California." Transactions of the Commonwealth Club of California 21, no. 3 (June 8, 1926):101–52.

Kelsey, C. E. Report to the Commissioner of Indian Affairs, Washington, D.C. Sacramento: Bureau of Indian Affairs, Department of the Interior, August 8, 1905.

Keyes, E. D. Fifty Years' Observations of Man and Events, Civil and Military. New York: Charles Scribner's Sons, 1884.

Kinsman, Joe. "Reminiscences." Madera County Magazine 1915, 1.

———. "The Story of Joe Kinsman, Pioneer." Madera County Magazine 1, no. 1 (1915):16–19.

Klette, William. "Lieutenant Skeane: California's Forgotten Hero." True West (June 1992):52–55.

Kroeber, A. L. Handbook of the Indians of California. New York: Dover, 1976.

Lamb, Sidney MacDonald. "Northfork Mono Grammar." Ph.D. dissertation, University of California, Graduate Division, Northern Section, 1958.

Latta, Frank. Handbook of the Yokuts Indians. Santa Cruz: Bear State Books, 1977.

Leother, Christopher. "Western Mono Mythology: A Numic Oral Tradition in California." Paper presented at the Great Basin Anthropological Conference, Reno, October 1990.

Miller, J. M. "'Peagie' Trenches in Which the Monos Trapped Their Suppers." *Yosemite Nature Notes,* 6, no. 1 (1927):6–7.

Mitchell, Annie R. *Jim Savage and the Tulareno Indians.* Tucson: Westernlore Press, 1957.

Muir, John. *My First Summer in the Sierra.* Boston: Houghton Mifflin, 1911.

Muñoz, Neva Jeanne Harkins. "Political Middlemanship and the Double Bind: James D. Savage and the Fresno River Reservation." Ph.D. dissertation, University of California, Riverside, 1980.

Noble, W. B. "A Day with the Mono Indians" (1904). In *A Collection of Ethnographical Articles of the California Indians,* edited by Robert F. Heizer, 42–46. Ramona, Calif.: Ballena Press Publications in Archaeology, Ethnology, and History, no. 7 (1976).

Norris, Evan. "A Syntactic Sketch of Mono." Master's thesis, California State University, Fresno, 1976.

Perlot, Jean-Nicholas. *Gold Seeker: Adventures of a Belgian Argonaut During the Gold Rush Years.* Edited by R. Lamar. New Haven: Yale University Press, 1985.

Pietroforte, Alfred. "Songs of the Yokuts and Paiutes." *Naturegraph,* 1965.

Redinger, David H. *The Story of Big Creek.* Glendale, Calif.: Trans-Anglo Books, 1986.

Russell, Carl P. "Geography of the Mariposa Indian War." *Yosemite Nature Notes* 30 (1951):22, 24–30, 53–56, 63–71.

———. *100 Years in Yosemite.* Berkeley: University of California Press, 1947.

———. "Unique Food of Monos." *Yosemite Nature Notes* 6, no. 3 (March 31, 1927):23–24.

Scheidt, William A. "A History of the Hidden Reservoir Area, Fresno River, California." Prepared for the National Park Service, Department of the Interior and the Corps of Engineers, United States Army, September 15, 1966.

Scovel, Doris. *The Fortune Seekers.* Fresno: Pioneer Publishing Co., 1981.

Shinn, Charles H. "Old Man Chepo." *Craftsman Magazine* (1912):622–30.

Sierra National Forest. "History of the Ross Cabin." Pamphlet. North Fork: Minarets Ranger District, n.d.

Solnit, Rebecca. "Up the River of Mercy." *Sierra* (November–December 1992): 50–57.

Spier, Robert F. G. "Monache." In *Handbook of American Indians.* Vol. 8: California, edited by Robert F. G. Heizer, 426–36. Washington, D.C.: Smithsonian Institution, 1978.

U.S. Army. *Reports of Acting Superintendents, U.S. Army Headquarters, Yosemite National Park.* Yosemite: Yosemite Research Library, 1896, 1897.

Wogaman, Emily. *Medicine Man to Medic: A Tribute to Annie Kinsman Flores and Granddaughter Marcella M. Flores, M.D., Mono Indians of Madera, California.* Madera, Calif.: Sierra Star Press, 1973.

INDEX